I AM THAT UNICORN

MEMOIR OF AN INDONESIAN QUEER

AROZAK SALAM

Some names and identifying details have been changed to protect their identity. The majority events in this book take place from 2010 to 2017.

First published in 2023
Text and copyright © Arozak Salam, 2023
All rights reserved. No part of this publication may be reproduced without prior permission of the publisher.

That Unicorn
Perth, Western Australia
Web: thatunicorn.com

We acknowledge the Traditional Owners of the Country on which we live and work. We pay our respects to all Aboriginal and Torres Strait Islander Elders, past and present.

 A catalogue record for this book is available from the National Library of Australia

ISBN 9780645843606 (paperback)
ISBN 9780645843613 (ebook)

Cover images   : Deric Martin
Cover design   : Romain Gambetta

I AM THAT UNICORN

MEMOIR OF AN INDONESIAN QUEER

To the lost souls.
Somewhere out there,
your tribe is waiting for you.

Everything will make sense.
You are just imperfectly beautiful.

All this time.

CONTENTS

1	The Clue	1
2	The First Sight	11
3	The Counterpart	21
4	The One-Way Ticket	32
5	The Life from Zero	41
6	The Festival	50
7	The West Coast	60
8	The Job	68
9	The Wedding	78
10	The Marching Boys	87
11	The Circle of Friends	95
12	The Engineer	103
13	The Asian	112
14	The Gay Trip	120
15	The Blazing Swan	130
16	The Pageant	139
17	The Visa	149

18	The Costumes	158
19	The Boylesque	166
20	The International Debut	176
21	The Redundancy	186
22	The Oppression	196
23	The Invitation	205
24	The Ceremony	213
	Acknowledgments	
	About the author	

1 THE CLUE

Neon lights, confetti, low-lying fog, and the intro of "Crazy in Love" by Beyoncé. I like a grand entrance to begin my show as a unicorn burlesque performer. But that is a story for later. I am going to start my opening chapter with a confession instead. When I was five years old, I used to play a Power Ranger character with my friends. I liked to untuck my shirt, turn it into a crop top showing my belly button, and push the boys as I walked, "I am a Pink Ranger."

Being a Pink Ranger in the biggest Muslim population in the world, Indonesia, meant I had to endure being called *bencong* in my childhood. I was just a boy who liked to express my creativity in a brightly coloured outfit, but I was already being labelled as gay before I knew what it meant. Not until I was in junior high school did I understand the same-sex attraction after having a crush on my classmate. What I saw was an imperfection. My sexual orientation brought down on me a guilt that emanated from my raw interpretation of a page in the Quran saying that gay men belong to hell. I blamed my five-year-old self for choosing a Pink Power Ranger character. It made me gay, I thought.

Throughout my adolescence, I wondered who I would be if I were not a Pink Ranger. But my rebellious inner voice often provoked me to think that maybe I was meant to be a Pink Ranger. I was trapped in my own battles to find such answers, which left me contemplating as I approached my early twenties. Maybe the Pink Ranger was a major life clue. Maybe it was a sign leading me to discover the core of my identity and explore the part of me outside my society bubble.

There I was, deciding to pursue life's clues. After finishing university, I went solo backpacking through Southeast Asia for five weeks while my freshly graduated peers were busy looking for jobs. This was 2010, and the idea of travelling alone overseas was uncommon for Indonesians. My itineraries were filled with exploration of gay bars and meeting up with local gay people in every country I visited. I let myself be the Pink Ranger I had always wanted to be and embraced every moment of soul-searching. I did not tell anyone about my first gay adventure as I was still in the closet. To my family and friends, I was adventurous. To me, I was adventurously fabulous.

"How were the girls in Thailand?" my friend asked me while he stroked his beard.

"Did you end up with a ladyboy?" He winked.

Backpacking around Southeast Asia was a breakthrough as I encountered plenty of Pink Ranger boys out there while I got to know myself even more. I hoped to become a new me after graduating from my adventure, but I could not deal with the reality I knew I would face once I returned home. I came back to living as a discreet gay man—my sexual orientation was a burden due to societal and religious pressures in my circle of family and friends. I still could not fully embrace my inner Pink Ranger.

"Any luck with job hunting?" My mom was checking on me at my study desk before she went to bed.

I gave her a half-shrug as my default response. It would be too bitter to say there was nothing new to report, and I did not want to disappoint my mom every time I looked at her. I wished she could see through my eyes that I was dealing not only with job hunting but also identity searching. Any sign from the universe would help, as I had been jobless for months amid invisible life directions. Many of my friends had gotten jobs right after graduation. If it was a race, I was still tying my shoelaces while they had already started running. My self-confidence was dissipating day by day. I wanted to avoid socialising and dodging the questions from people about my life after the Southeast Asia backpacking trip. During one sleepless night though, I found what I believed was a clue as to what my next journey might be.

"*Are you the chosen one?*" was advertised on the poster online.

***

The Ministry of Youth and Sport of the Republic of Indonesia launched a prestigious youth exchange program allowing the nation's youth to represent the country. The initial selections were conducted at the provincial level. The government of West Java, where I lived, organised three stages of selection covering administration, a judging panel and quarantine to accommodate approximately 500 applicants.

"*Please rank your preference for the youth exchange program, with country destinations as follows: Canada, Japan, Malaysia, Korea and Australia,*" read the instructions on the form.

I ignored the application for days because I did not have standout academic and extracurricular achievements. I thought about failing even before the selection started. But I flashed back to being a Pink Ranger and how I'd felt liberated unlocking myself as an openly gay traveller during the Southeast Asia trip. This youth exchange program could be my jackpot as I continued exploring my identity. I had to do something to flip my destiny, as no one would do it but me.

"Hello, everyone! I would like to discuss the impact of social media on youth nowadays…" After passing the administrative stage, I delivered the presentation to the judging panel based on the script I had prepared beforehand. My English was not fluent at that time. Speaking for three minutes was the accumulation of a week of effort to memorise the words and rehearse in front of the mirror. I created simple traditional dance choreography for the cultural performance assessment and presented it as a flash mob where anybody could follow my lead, like in an aerobics class. During the interview, solo backpacking through Southeast Asia became my selling point to prove I could be flexible in new cultures.

"I will always have the option to go to other parts of the world as a tourist. However, to go abroad representing Indonesia as a youth ambassador under the Ministry of Youth and Sport of the Republic of Indonesia will be a once-in-a-lifetime opportunity." I made eye contact with the interviewers.

"Besides, I believe having an endless curiosity for a new adventure is contagious. I want to share this spirit with the people around me so that every youth can be inspired by the adventurous tales of others. There are more stories in life than being born, studying, getting married, having kids and dying," I explained. My heart was beating fast.

Only 25 candidates were invited to the final round. I had

previously failed in the very first round of the *Indonesian Idol* auditions. Progressing to the last stage of youth exchange selection was already a big achievement for me.

"Welcome to the final leg of the youth exchange program selection." A man with a *Batik* shirt—an Indonesian technique of applying wax-resistant dye to cloth—spoke to the candidates on the opening night of quarantine. "As part of the assessment, you will face different challenges. You should be ready for a focus group discussion, talent performance, in-depth interview, and written test." He pointed his finger to remind us that we would face a tough selection process.

Some people were eliminated on the first night, and I was humbled to survive until the day of the announcement. There were 15 high-achieving and talented candidates left. Some spoke four foreign languages, played various musical instruments, and had won sports competitions. We gathered in the room waiting for the final verdict. It was a dead silence, but my mind screamed out loud, wanting to end the suspense.

"All of you are the future of the youth movement. You have shown us your best efforts during the quarantine," said the head officer of Youth and Sports Affairs of West Java at the closing speech.

"This year, our province received the quota from the Ministry of Youth and Sports Affairs of the Republic of Indonesia: one male for the Australia Indonesia Youth Exchange Program (AIYEP), one male for the Canada Indonesia Youth Exchange Program (ICYEP), and one female for The Ship for the Southeast Asian and Japanese Youth Program (SSEAYP)." His eyes focused on the piece of paper in his hand.

Every year, the central government organises a quota system

for each province to send their representatives. Depending on the designated youth exchange countries, the Indonesian contingent consists of between 18 and 26 delegates, half male and half female. Canada was my first option because it had the longest exchange duration, about six months. Australia was at the bottom of my wish list. I did not know much about the country, despite it having the most prominent gay pride celebration in the southern hemisphere, Sydney Mardi Gras. Australia was a mysterious country to me.

"For the AIYEP delegate, congratulations to…" He paused briefly. "Arozak Salam." His voice boomed across the room.

The silence converted to the explosion of clapping hands. The candidate beside me tapped my shoulder to signal that my name was being called. I could not hide my smile, but deep down, I giggled incredulously. "Australia?"

***

AIYEP was established in 1981 as an initiative of the Australia-Indonesia Institute Department of Foreign Affairs and Trade. Since then, the alumni of AIYEP have always arranged the national pre-departure training in Jakarta to share their experiences and help the newly selected delegates bond as one solid team.

"Remember that you are still a candidate, and we can send you back to your province if there is any misconduct." The alumni coordinator stood before us, looking so vibrant with her red skirt and lipstick.

"No one is guaranteed to go to Australia until the day we send you to the airport," she added.

The pressure was on, but my excitement kept me alive as I believed I was on the right track, following life's clues. There was this déjà vu feeling when I sat in the conference room. I could sense something big was about to happen. It felt like I was in my own movie scene, and all the surrounding people were there to convince me that I would get through the upcoming puzzling plots.

"You will spend two months in Australia and two months in Indonesia with the Australian representatives. We will discuss various topics this week. All the presentation materials are tailored to minimise the problems that usually occur during the program. We do not want to hear of unnecessary drama later on." She looked at me.

I smiled back at her to be polite while adjusting the black feather brooch that I'd pinned on my white shirt. I wanted to look fabulous, even at 2 pm.

"Tomorrow you will learn how to handle the culture shock in Australia, and reverse culture shock when you return here." She read the rundown of the pre-departure training on the projector.

"The rest of the week, you will learn public speaking for a courtesy call with the Australian and Indonesian governments, and how to interact with the Australian delegates when they join you. This is the most serious part; we will discuss how to organise community development in rural areas in Indonesia, setting the host family's expectations, internship and cultural performance at the schools in Australia and Indonesia. You all got it?" She clapped her hands once to grab our attention.

The room was silent. I looked at the candidate beside me, who struggled to open his eyes. I was not the only one who needed a double shot of coffee that afternoon.

The main challenge in uniting all 18 delegates was eliminating our individual egos as we came from different provinces and walks of life. We went through various group simulations to bond, like in military exercises. There was a blindfolded session for a half-day, so half of the group took care of the other. There was a session where we walked across two metres of burning coals and wood embers to overcome our internal fears. We spent sleepless nights practising for the *Saman* dance, where we lined up, sat on our heels and knelt in tight rows to create a fast-paced rhythm and collective group harmony.

The most anticipated activity during the training was when we got invited to meet Andi Mallarangeng, the Minister for Youth Affairs and Sports of the Republic of Indonesia. My pride as a civilian skyrocketed at having the opportunity to meet government officials.

"Take a picture with him," my dad texted me, as he and Andi Mallarangeng come from the same province, South Sulawesi.

After two hours of waiting in his office, he finally showed up to give us a send-off speech.

"Please remember that each of you will represent Indonesia, and you are the agents of change. Use this opportunity very well." He shook our hands one by one before taking a group photo.

After one week of pre-departure training, all 18 Australia Indonesia Youth Exchange Program delegates gathered on the inauguration night. The Indonesian flag was erected in the middle of the meeting room, and we walked past to kiss it one by one as part of the ceremonial procession.

"It's your turn." My friend Putri from Borneo Island pointed her finger.

I stepped up to the front and paused as I looked at the red and white flag. It reminded me of all the struggles I had been through. After returning from backpacking, I was hiding my identity as a Pink Ranger, had been unemployed for months, and had participated in a long youth exchange selection process. There had been no shortcuts to finally reaching this life's clue. It had started with one click to upload the application form, and there I was, standing in front of the national identity.

My right hand reached gently for the edge of the flag, and I held it to my lips. My vision started to get blurry, holding my emotions at the edge of my eyelids. I blinked, and tears fell on my cheeks. I felt honoured to be representing my country, Indonesia.

At the airport the next day, we all wore formal uniforms and a *peci*, the type of cap worn by the first president of Indonesia, Soekarno. The Indonesian national symbol, *Garuda*, was pinned on the left side of the *peci*. The outfit reminded us that we flew as youth ambassadors, not just travellers.

The alumni coordinator walked us to the international departure gate. "I am proud of you all, and please take care of each other in Australia. We can only assist you up to this point, and you are the ones who have the power to write your bilateral history during this program. We will see you again in two months here, together with the Australian contingent." She waved as the Indonesian contingent prepared to leave.

I looked at the sky from the plane window as we took off. Seeing Jakarta from the cloudy horizon was surreal. Looking back, I was flying not only to mark the new adventure that had just begun, but also to fetch my serendipity. It was calling me on a subtle frequency, and would lead to stories of broken-hearted immigration survival, a unicorn alter-ego, the world stage spotlight, and a reconciliation between religion, family and societal oppression. I did not know those remarkable events were waiting for me. My part was to take the first leap, boarding the flight that carried my life's clue.

I was wide awake on the plane, stomping my foot every now and then, realising I was about to spend two months in Australia. It was a country I had never thought I would ever visit, but Australia was about to change my life, from up above to down under.

2 THE FIRST SIGHT

"G'day, mate!" I tried pronouncing "mate" in an Australian accent just before the plane landed.

"Say M and 8 altogether. *M8!*" Putri, who sat next to me, moved her lips.

It was the spring of 2010 when I arrived in Brisbane, Queensland. My first impression of Australia was beautiful in purple. The blooming jacaranda trees welcomed us, and the purple leaves were scattered all over the pavement. It was an exotic sight for a tropical boy like me.

The Indonesian contingent spent a month in Brisbane as the initial phase of the youth exchange program. The first week of city orientation was a honeymoon. Coming from a developing country, simple things about Australia felt like a luxury. Tasting the fish and chips. Cycling around the botanical gardens. Enjoying the city view from the Wheel of Brisbane. Taking a boat trip along the Brisbane River at Southbank. My only mistake was spreading too much Vegemite on my bread, thinking it was a chocolate jam.

Each delegate stayed at local family houses to allow for daily cultural exchange with Australians. We gathered every

Monday at different Australian schools for cultural performances. The work placement filled our schedule for the rest of the week, allowing us to gain local job experience that matched our educational backgrounds. All these activities were designed as part of people-to-people diplomacy, an interaction between regular citizens of two countries at various levels to establish communication and understanding. The grassroots of cross-cultural exchange are basically in everyone's hands.

"We might not be born to perform, but we will conquer the stage!" I said to the team at our first cultural performance at Harristown State High School.

"Yes, we can!" Our hands were on top of each other as we yelled the performance's mantra backstage.

I had been chosen as the cultural performance coordinator for the Indonesian contingent. None of us were professional performers. Most delegates were students; the rest worked as accountants, flight attendants, engineers and scientists. But we wanted to make permanent memories, as our time in Australia was temporary. Apart from the official Monday schedule at the schools, we also thrived on performing at additional gigs. We dared to exchange our stage fright for the excitement of promoting Indonesian culture to the Australian audience.

"Guys! Have you heard of the concept of busking before?" I put a guitar case out while we gathered in Southbank Park.

It was a spontaneous idea to spice up the rehearsal. A few pedestrians started to pay attention as we made loud vocal sounds during the *Saman* dance. Some of them stood next to the guitar case and dropped coins into it. The money had pumped our performance's adrenaline that afternoon. We danced, following the percussion with a much faster tempo than usual.

"How much money did we get?" I asked Putri at the end of our rehearsal.

"Just $13!" She gave a bitter laugh. "There's 18 of us; not even a dollar each!"

"Oh well! After all, it's the Australian dollar, not the rupiah!" I recalculated the coins.

"Let's put it on a frame!" She grabbed my wrist. "For the memories we've earned by using our talent!"

On a separate occasion, the Indonesian contingent also performed a *Saman* dance for a fundraising event at Park Ridge Baptist Church, located 30 kilometres south of Brisbane. The dance itself actually contains a moral message of Islam and is typically performed to celebrate an Islamic event, such as the birthday of the prophet Muhammad.

"*Assalamualaikum,*" said our lead singer at the start of the *Saman* dance, wishing peace to the audience at the church.

The crowd went silent when the dance commenced. Some guests sitting at the circular tables shifted their bodies to observe the performance on the stage. They clapped as we delivered the fast-paced choreography. A few even forgot to turn off their camera flashes when taking photos. That night, we proved that art performance knows no boundaries, and bridges the differences between people from different backgrounds.

***

My host family in Brisbane was originally from New Zealand. As a 23-year-old guy from Indonesia who had never lived abroad before, I immediately encountered culture shock at the beginning of my stay with them. It took almost an hour by bus from where I stayed in Kenmore to get to my internship location in the city centre. After I did the morning prayer, I usually used the early hour to have breakfast with no rush and to get ready. One day, my host mum interrupted me in the kitchen.

"Do you know what time it is?" she whispered.

"Oh, it is 5.30 am," I answered with a smile.

"I know! Keep the noise down then!"

I thought she was genuinely asking for the time. Apparently, I had made too much noise when I'd washed my dirty cereal bowl. After that, I used a plastic spoon to avoid the clinking noise of metal tapping the bowl. I tiptoed around the house like a thief. I kept my time in the bathroom to under five minutes, brushing my teeth and splashing my face. My morning routine in Australia taught me to be a proficient silent ninja trying not to wake up the dragon.

The second culture shock I had was because of the rice. I craved it badly that I attempted to cook it by myself for the first time. As a result, I burned the pot.

"I bought something for you." My host mum handed me a rice cooker.

"Oh, wow!" I jumped off the floor.

"Thank you!" she quipped. Her tone of voice changed. I immediately realised she was being sarcastic, as I had not thanked her. I did not mean to be ungrateful. Quite the opposite; I was too overwhelmed.

"Thank you… Linda." I fixed my posture and spoke to her in a flat tone.

I looked at the rice cooker feeling guilty. In a split second, I remembered what the alumni had said during pre-departure training: "There are three magic expressions you should not forget in Australia: 'sorry', 'please', and 'thank you'!"

My zero-cooking-skill disasters did not stop with burning the rice. It was the first time I'd used a microwave. As I stayed with another Indonesian delegate at the house, I once saw her cooking noodles in the microwave. Feeling inspired, I also cooked instant noodles with a bit of improvisation. I added a raw egg to the bowl and put it in for five minutes. I went to my room while waiting for the timer.

Boom! I heard an explosion from the kitchen.

I was trembling when I opened the microwave. The egg had burst into pieces and was scattered inside. I cleaned it carefully to make sure there was no trace of the yolk. That egg bomb tragedy traumatised me, and I never went near the microwave again. Thank God I was alone in the house that day. If my host mum had found out about it, she probably would have given me a red card, banning me from her kitchen forever.

Despite the culture shock that happened predominantly in the kitchen, I knew that my host family cared for me. They cooked vegan foods, attended our cultural performance, and took me for a weekend getaway to the Gold Coast. Knowing they treated me fairly as an adult, I did not hesitate to communicate with them about my specific request. I intentionally planned this time as part of my self-discovery while I was in Brisbane.

"Can I go out tonight to check out Brisbane's nightlife?" I went to the living room where my host parents spent their Saturday nights together.

"By yourself?" my host mum gasped.

There was a silent moment for a couple of seconds. I fidgeted, waiting for her next words.

"As a paramedic, I know the area so well." She held her

breath. "There are lots of drunk people. Are you sure you want to go?" She inclined her head, trying to change my mind.

"Yes! It is part of my cultural observation," I smirked.

"What if your passport gets stolen or something bad happens?"

"He will be fine," my host dad interrupted her.

I felt relieved knowing somebody had backed me up. I took a moment trying to convince my host mum. "I will take care of myself, I promise."

"Well, you are an adult. It is up to you." She lowered her voice.

"Just be careful." My host dad gave me the green light.

Besides having a cultural exchange with my host family, I also had a hidden agenda to visit a gay bar. Whilst I had been to Southeast Asia, I also wanted to experience the gay scene in a developed country like Australia. It was an important mission for me, as every step of exploration was progress towards accepting my identity as a gay man.

My venture was a go. I took the train and arrived at Fortitude Valley, only to find out that my host mum was utterly right. I was terrified to see many drunk people screaming and shouting on the street. I was scared that if something terrible happened that night, the youth exchange coordinator would terminate my stay and send me back to Indonesia for misconduct. I rushed to avoid eye contact, raised my chest to toughen my look and pretended I knew where I was going. It was difficult, as my basic phone was only for calling and texting. Like in the old days, the paper map guided me to the gay bar.

It was called The Wickham. I walked a few laps around the block to make up my mind as I was still reluctant to go inside. I saw people going into the bar one by one, and I decided to follow them. I needed to use the toilet as the temperature outside had dropped.

The remixed pop music welcomed me when I entered. It lifted my mood and reduced my nerves about coming to the gay bar alone. I started to boogie, but did not stop checking out the bar's atmosphere. I stole a glance at the guys in front of me, holding hands and sometimes exchanging passionate kisses. I would not have had a clue they were gay had I not seen them sharing affection with each other at the bar.

I had a parallel vision between what I was seeing and my memories of gay life in Indonesia. At home, there was pressure to be reserved, and no space to show public affection; otherwise, people would spread gossip to colleagues or, worse, to family members. But standing in the gay bar in Brisbane made me realise that affection is supposed to be a blessing and not something to be suppressed. Affection is there to be embraced. It is a feeling and a beautiful thing; without it, life is just monochrome.

That night, I contemplated in the middle of the crowd.

If I live here, will I be living a double life?
Will I still freak out on the way to the gay bar?
Will my heart feel guilty if I kiss a guy on the street?
Will I be able to bring a guy home casually?
Will I ever have a chance to live here though?

"A glass of orange juice, please!" I said to the bartender, before jumping onto the dance floor. Although completely sober, I pretended I was drunk enough to dance. I kept dancing until the bar closed, as I thought it would be my last time in a gay bar in Australia.

***

After staying in Brisbane for a month, the Indonesian contingent travelled to Roma, Queensland. The second phase of the youth exchange program started in a rural area. All the delegates continued the same activities, such as living with a host family, cultural performance and work placement. The only different thing was that we immersed ourselves in the outback lifestyle. Brisbane was already a quiet place compared to my hometown, Bandung, which has a population of 8.5 million. When I found out that Roma only had around seven thousand people, I wondered if I was the only gay in town.

I stayed with a beautiful couple who owned a mining business. Every morning when we had breakfast in the kitchen, my host parents shared a passionate kiss to start the day. It was like watching an intense kiss in the war movies when a soldier was about to leave his wife before going into battle. The kind of intimacy that was more than a one-second kiss on the lips. It might have been usual for them, but it was a culture shock for me. Instead of listening to the smooch sound in the background, I learned how to not stare at them and just focused on counting my cereal in the bowl.

My room was located just next to theirs. As the house was built high on the land and supported by a wooden floor, any footsteps could be heard. One time, I woke up in the middle of the night as I could feel the wooden floor shaking, and it was not an earthquake. I realised they were making love next door when I heard the occasional moan. I decided not to move my sleeping position at all because I was afraid to make a cracking noise from my spring bed, a signal that I was awake. I forced myself to close my eyes and ears, finding my inner peace, thinking it was just another cultural immersion experience in Australia.

Living the outback lifestyle for three weeks marked the last activities for the Indonesian contingent in Australia. Two hours before we left Roma, I decided to do my own farewell procession.

"Let's bury our secret messages here." I pointed at the biggest tree in a grassy field.

"You dig the soil first then." Putri handed me a trowel.

"Sure." I showed my biceps to her. "Meanwhile, you can start writing your wishes." I gave her the pen and paper.

"This reminds me of a scene in a soap opera," she giggled.

"The power of the dream." I raised both hands as I looked at the sky.

I took a deep breath, feeling content before I walked back to my host family's house. The box containing my aspirations was planted just a week before Christmas. The first wish was to get a monthly engineering salary of $5,000, followed by finding a husband before turning forty. Last but not least, I wanted to be back in Australia within five years. I knew that somewhere beyond the seventh sky, the universe would make those wishes come true in a perfect timeline. It would work in an absurd algorithm of life that I could not yet foresee.

Australia had never been in my plan before, but my first impression was profound. I'd met inspiring people within two months, including government officials, local families, workers, students, and strangers on the street. The people-to-people diplomacy shaped unforgettable moments and built a special place at the core of my heart. My culture shock experiences, from vegemite to kitchen madness, were the additional reasons I fell in love with Australia. And the discovery of the local gay bar in Brisbane inspired me to further explore my identity.

I had experienced the real Australian spirit that is welcoming, laidback and friendly. I was not ready to leave the Land Down Under, as I carried heavy, sweet memories. However, I was at peace knowing I'd left my wishes beneath one foot of Australian outback soil.

3 THE COUNTERPART

Two countries across the ocean, two strangers from different borders. Their stories merged into one eventually.

The Indonesian delegates returned to Brisbane to meet the Australian participants for the first time before visiting Indonesia as a whole group. We had a week of joint orientation to discuss the community development plan, cultural performance collaboration, and accommodation arrangements. However, one Australian delegate pulled out of the program due to health reasons. The youth exchange organiser could not find a replacement at the last minute. The male Australian composition became an odd number.

"Can you join our team, please?" Tania, the Australian cultural performance coordinator, asked me. "We need to pair up for our dance formation."

"You know I love performing." I strutted in front of her.

"Also, I love your collaboration ideas." Tania gave me a high five, agreeing with my proposal for a joint cultural performance, which I had prepared long before orientation started.

We sang a medley of *"Burung Kakak Tua"* and the "Kookaburra Sits in the Old Gumtree" song, symbolising the bird species from each country. It was followed by the second collaboration, a musical instrument jam session using a didgeridoo representing Australia and a set of *angklung* representing Indonesia. We translated the bilateral relationship between Indonesia and Australia through melody and choreography, a soft diplomacy dispatch from the stage to the audience.

The Australian delegates' odd number also impacted the counterpart arrangement. Ideally, a pair of Australian and Indonesian delegates of the same gender would stay together with a host family in Indonesia. One of the Indonesian male participants technically would not have a counterpart, but the organiser had to join him with another pair so as to have a three-way set-up. The arrangement process was conducted through group activities to observe our personalities. It was like a dating show to find the right match. Everyone could propose a wish list to the organiser with their potential counterpart's name, but I like surprises and let them match me instead.

The pairings were announced on the last day of orientation, and I was thrilled to find out which Australian delegate had been assigned as my counterpart. Andrew was a guy I'd spotted sweaty in the hallway after returning from an afternoon run. I had often kept my eyes on him during the cultural performance as his position on stage was next to mine. He was an athletic bloke from Sydney who had lived in Bali for several months. He was a charming fellow who would change the whole narration of my love life.

"I will give you new vocabulary daily to improve your Indonesian language." I wrote the first word in his notebook.

"*Bahagia?*" Andrew asked.

"It means happy, the feeling of having you as my counterpart," I told him.

***

Wakatobi Islands, located in Southeast Sulawesi Province, Indonesia, hosted the next phase of AIYEP. On New Year's Eve, all the delegates were invited to a welcome dinner at the mayor's house.

"You know, I participated in AIYEP too, back in 1987!" said Hugua, Wakatobi's mayor.

We spent our New Year's Eve having a long, nostalgic conversation with him instead of watching fireworks or attending a celebration with local people on the beach.

After midnight, Andrew and I returned to our host family. We stayed in the same room and shared a bed that perfectly fitted us. It was the first time we'd spent the night together. We lay down talking about what we could have done on New Year's Eve.

Our pillow talks slowly faded into a tranquil moment. The night was quiet, but my mind was the opposite. I tried to close my eyes, but I was far from dreamland. We touched each other occasionally as we adjusted our sleeping positions. The darkness had made us more physically intimate, and we lay hand in hand. Andrew grabbed my thigh to get me closer. The bed had little space, so I rolled my body to be on top of his. We paused while staring closely at each other's lips. Our warm breath was out of control, and so were our heartbeats when both chests were in contact. One, two, and three seconds, then we finally kissed. It started with one short kiss in silence and transformed into long aggressive lips, full of testosterone. Time froze; it was like having New Year's Eve fireworks in my mouth. It blew me away.

I did not know my counterpart was into men until that first night. The next day, I brought the conversation around to sexual orientation and shared my experiences, including being discreet around my family and friends.

"I've never had frequent intimacy with men. But I always knew I was attracted to them." Andrew lay down beside me. "I mentioned it to my parents before joining the youth exchange program. Some Australian participants know that I fancy men, and they're completely fine with it," he added.

I now had a counterpart and a romance. Sometimes we spent morning time cuddling until our host dad, La Bauna, knocked on the door to notify us that breakfast was ready. He treated us like his sons, talking about his life over a hot coffee. La Bauna's wife always sat separately in the kitchen while we were eating. Later, I found out that she only grabbed food after we had finished, showing respect to the guests, which was a new culture for me, coming from West Java province.

We often hung out with Surya, La Bauna's son. One afternoon, he came up to us.

"Do you want to visit a shipwreck?" he asked.

"Only if we can see the sunset from there," I replied.

"Let's take my traditional canoe!" He took us to the pier.

I have a great memory from our time at the shipwreck, one more beautiful than the orange sky in the dusk. It was when Andrew and I jumped together from the edge of the ship and screamed at the top of our lungs. The first thing I saw when I broke through the water's surface was his curly hair, blue eyes and charming smile.

"Woohoo! I feel so alive!" he shouted.

My head was above the water, but I was drowned by his baritone voice.

The evenings were when we bonded with the kids from La

Bauna's extended family. Together, we were like parents raising children. I played the guitar, and Andrew taught them English. We both came up with new songs every night. Sometimes the kids were too excited. It always ended up chaotic in the living room; they pushed each other to decide who would sing first. They loved to play with us and brought their 15 friends to sing and dance throughout the night. The girls became so enthusiastic when the national broadcasting company documented our English class at La Bauna's home. They put excessive make-up on, thinking they would become celebrities that evening.

There is a local love celebration in Wakatobi called *Kabuenga*. The ceremony is intended for matchmaking between a male and a female. It was originally for sailors who wanted to meet the local girls and become their partners. *"Kabuenga"* means "giant swing". The proposed couple sit on the swing, and the people pushing them from behind pray and sing a folklore song. They believe that a couple who attends a *Kabuenga* ceremony is destined for each other.

All 35 delegates from Australia and Indonesia were invited to take part in the *Kabuenga* celebration. Each of us was given a chance to pick our partner from the opposite gender to sit together on the swing.

"Do you want to go with me?" I asked Andrew after I did the ceremony with my Indonesian friend, Putri.

Our host dad and all the kids witnessed the moment we were swinging in the *Kabuenga* ceremony. They had never seen two men sitting together at *Kabuenga* before and thought we were just playing around to have fun. We both held onto the swing while the kids pushed us from the back. They were laughing as the swing got faster. Under Wakatobi's sky, I sat beside him, wishing for love magic.

The emotional connection between us was getting deeper than ever. But we hid our intimacy from our cohort. I respected Andrew's privacy. But it was hard to pretend nothing was happening, especially during group activities. The intimate time we spent together meant something to me. I wished I could share my romance stories with my friends. I wanted it to be told casually in conversation, without second-guessing whether it would be acceptable.

One afternoon, we were supposed to go to the beach together with La Bauna's son, who had prepared fishing gear and picnic equipment. However, Andrew bailed without any notice and disappeared for the whole day. I had a mixed reaction when he came home later that night. I was carrying the burden of our hidden affection.

"I think it's better if we just stay as counterparts without having any romance between us." My voice trembled as I spoke to him. "Surya kept asking where you were, but I had no idea. He had already prepared for the outing, you know!"

"Sorry. I went to lunch with some of my Indonesian friends." He looked down.

"You could have told me rather than disappearing. Why are you hiding where you go anyway?"

There are moments in life when I say I want to quit, but I do not mean it. Sometimes it is just an impulsive reaction because I am upset. The conversation with Andrew was like that; it was just friction between two people who had gotten together. Without a doubt, I wanted to keep our romance going. It was hard to keep it discreet, but we still shared physical intimacy, even after our heart-to-heart chat that night.

But things began to change between us. It all started at a program break just before all the delegates travelled to the last phase in Kendari City. The Indonesian and Australian contingents visited a resort for two nights, where I shared a bungalow with Andrew. During the day, I spent time with some Indonesian friends to give him space to hang out with his Australian mates. But we still spent the first night together.

The next day, I took a boat trip to another island to buy a couple of beers for our drinking game. When I returned to our bungalow that night, he was not there. I waited for him until I fell asleep. Meanwhile, the whole island had a blackout due to insufficient generator energy during a storm.

The slammed door woke me up in the middle of the night. I had not locked the door as I'd expected my counterpart to come back at some point. It had been a restless evening, spent wondering where he was. Only the view of the sunrise could calm me down. When the heavy rain stopped, I contemplated at the pier until the boat picked all of us up a couple of hours later, ending the holiday with a heavy feeling.

"Something is not right. Why did he leave me alone last night?" I cried on Putri's shoulder on the ship.

For the first time, I told my romance stories to one of the youth exchange participants.

"He did not even talk to me right now! As if nothing happened!" I sobbed.

"I heard a rumour," Putri said. "Apparently Andrew stayed over at Adam's bungalow last night."

***

The youth exchange program continued in Kendari City for a couple of weeks. The Australians commenced the internship program, while the Indonesian delegates assisted their counterparts at their workplace. Staying with a new host family in Kendari was the most challenging period. Although they accommodated us very well, night-time with Andrew was tough. Sharing a bed reminded me of our romance in Wakatobi Islands. There were still pillow talks but minus the physical intimacy.

When Andrew had a shower one morning, I noticed a message notification had popped up on his mobile. My logic told me to ignore the rumour about my counterpart and Adam, an Indonesian male delegate. But my heart burnt. I gave up on remaining sane as my evil side whispered to me to read what was in the inbox. It was an old phone, so I could access it without the passcode.

"I miss you too! Can't wait to see you this afternoon," read the text from Adam.

I rushed to the veranda to take in some fresh air. What I read had strangled me, and I felt like all the oxygen in the world had gone. I was the one who had told Andrew that we should just be counterparts without romance involved. But I did not expect he would date another guy while he was around me. There were red flags about the day he bailed for the prepared outing in Wakatobi and the night he had abandoned me in the bungalow. And it all made sense to me now: Andrew wanted to be with Adam. I became the one who was left out.

I still did my best at the worst time. I swallowed the pain and tried to be the best counterpart for Andrew during the rest of the program, knowing I had come so far to be a youth ambassador. I pretended that I did not know anything about his romance. I still taught him the Indonesian language and hung out with our host family. I helped him change his internship from a newspaper publisher to the Kendari mayor's office, which was more suitable for his international relations degree. It was my duty to be a helpful counterpart representing my country.

I slept with someone who gave me the sorrow. Every night we shared a bed, it felt like I had drunk a cup of poison. I felt so lonely lying next to him. Andrew did not tell me why he came home late most nights, and I never asked, although I knew he was spending time with Adam. The hardest part was that their romance was known publicly among the group. Meanwhile, the memories I had with him remained in the closet. The rumour circulating said that I was jealous because I could not be with my counterpart. But my peers did not understand how hard it was to create my own safe space while Andrew slept next to me. I smelled of his romance with someone else every night.

There were days when I got up and looked in the mirror. I thought I was the star of the youth exchange program by being a cultural performance coordinator and organising the collaboration with the Australian contingent. The fact that Andrew had chosen Adam made me realise I was that "too much" type of person. Someone who was too eager to get something and too sensitive to feel the emotion. Knowing Andrew had made up a reason for coming home late after celebrating Valentine's Day with Adam made me realise I was just pathetic. I'd spent every second that night waiting for him to come home so I could give him a box of chocolates I'd bought from the mall. But it ended up in the bin, as I was tired of my own need to prove to him that I was worth it.

The night after the youth exchange program finished, all

the delegates gathered in a hotel in Jakarta. I already knew that Andrew was sharing a bed with Adam that night. I was in my room alone and asked him to come over.

"Every moment I have with you is like a dream." I paused. "A nightmare, to be exact." I stared into his eyes while he remained in silence. "I will be back in my hometown tomorrow morning. And tonight, I am going to the nightclub with the other Australians." I opened my laptop as I spoke. "The surreal moments of these past couple of months will end soon, and you need to know that you hurt me badly! I am sure you realise that I am aware of what is going on between you and Adam." I stopped for a moment. "But I do not want to have any regrets. I have been compiling all the footage of us right from the beginning, not knowing the ending would be like this. But I have committed to finishing this video for my last task as your counterpart."

The hotel room remained quiet. I glanced at him and wondered about his reaction. Andrew sobbed while watching the video, which told me all I needed to know. I left him in the room without saying a single word.

When I was about to check out the next morning, my counterpart and Adam came to my hotel room.

"Can I help carry your luggage?" asked Andrew.

"I'm good, thanks." I ended the chat with no smile.

I went down to reception, where some Indonesian friends were waiting.

"Until we meet again," I repeatedly said to four Indonesian participants as a farewell.

My counterpart and Adam were there too. I was surprised they'd had the audacity to come together, side by side, before

I left. Seeing them together in the lobby was an awkward and painful moment. I hugged Adam to give him a farewell anyway because we were both Indonesian delegates, and I gave him a little mercy.

The last person left to farewell was Andrew. This was my last chance to throw the tantrum I had built up over the past month. I really wanted to swear in front of his face because I had been suppressing my anger. But I just took a deep, aching breath without making eye contact. I hugged him briefly as my friends watched what was happening between us. We were just in silence; neither of us had the urge to say any words.

That was the saddest thing. If there was anything to say, it should have come from his mouth, and this was his last chance to say something. If not an apology, at least a thank you after I'd assisted him in staying in Indonesia, or any words to indicate that what we'd had back then had meant something. But there was just a cold silence between us.

I got into the taxi without looking back. The sadness was excruciatingly deep to the point that I was numb. I wanted to cry, but nothing came from my eyes. I just stared blankly out the window.

I could never have imagined that the imbalance of the male delegate formation would cause me unforgettable despair at the end of the youth exchange program. I felt left out as if I had had no counterpart. My heart was full of bruises. I could not wait to get back home and sleep alone in my own bed—a safe space for me to heal, far away from him.

4 THE ONE-WAY TICKET

My first name is broken-hearted; my last name is culture shock. You can call me miserable.

I lived in a nostalgic world. Everything at home was the same as it had been when my life had been turned upside down by the youth exchange program. My dad still woke up at 4 am to do morning prayer. My mom still loved to cook fried rice for breakfast. My friends still explored new travel destinations on the weekend. My family and friends could not understand the intensity of the youth exchange memories I had. They only listened to the friction of stories that had happened in Brisbane and Wakatobi Islands. Social media was the oasis in which the ex-delegates consoled each other. Soon it became tragic. I saw my counterpart and Adam uploading the same Facebook profile pictures, holding hands and wearing the same shirt, full of joy. Their happy image online was my agony in real life.

"Your counterpart and Adam had a romantic farewell kiss at the airport," Putri told me over the phone. "Lucky you were not there because they kissed in front of everybody before the Australian delegates left Indonesia."

I unfriended them from Facebook for an instant remedy. But it did not heal me fully. I wished that broken-heartedness was a physical sickness. Something I could put a bandage on or glue any broken pieces together. I woke up every morning feeling something heavy inside me. The pain was absurd and invisible, but I felt it to the bone.

Life went on amid my lowest point. One week after finishing the youth exchange program, I got a job at a construction company. They assigned me to the new field development project on Sumatra Island. I was cast away to the middle of the jungle, staying in a dormitory room with ten other workers. Every morning at 6 am, a four-wheel drive drove us an hour's journey to the muddy field location, and we worked there for 12 hours. After dinner, around 8 pm, our accommodation turned into a hub of lonely people. I would go to the internet cafe next door to access gay chat websites while my co-workers called their families. My daily life was a repetition of these activities. There was no such thing as a weekend. Every day was a workday. At first, I enjoyed having the same routine as it meant I did not have to make any plans. But after a while, it made me dead internally. I started thinking about that night's sleep as soon as I woke up.

I shared my office with a co-worker who was two years younger than me. Often, in the morning, I listened to him complaining about being in the field project.

"I want to travel to different countries," he mumbled behind the desk. "Instead, I am stuck here in the middle of the jungle. Don't you think it's sad? We are still young!" He looked at me. "I don't want to give up my dreams, but I have no other option except working here; I need money."

There was an adventurous life outside the field project I

knew, which I could only reminisce about by looking at the sky from my office's window. I did not want to end up like my colleague, a young man who was able to imagine his dream but could not make it happen. I had to fight for my own freedom in the name of the Pink Ranger I had always been and my pact that was buried in Australian soil. I knew the story of my self-discovery in Australia should not stop in the youth exchange program chapter. There had to be more to come.

An exciting mission was ahead of me: finding a way back to Australia. I needed something to look forward to, and it allowed me to leave the broken-hearted monster behind. My daily life purpose was not just thinking about the night's sleep anymore. I felt alive again.

***

Crossing the country border to pursue my mission as a prospective immigrant from a developing country was not as easy as packing my luggage and booking a one-way ticket. The visa application process to go to any developed country is arduous even for a holiday, let alone to migrate. My first step started with a dull task. I filtered a lot of information on the Australian immigration portal about all types of visas and became an immigration agent for myself.

"*Subclass 476 Skilled – Recognised Graduate Visa.*" I found the information on the website. "*A temporary visa to stay for up to 18 months in Australia without any restriction on work, travel or study.*

"*To be eligible, the applicant shall be a recent graduate engineer or have graduated a maximum of two years ago from a recognised overseas university, completing a selected engineering degree as per the Australian high-skilled occupation list.*" I read the terms.

Having an Ocean Engineering degree opened up the possibility of returning to Australia. It was one of major studies at my university, the Institute of Technology of Bandung (ITB), that had been internationally accredited at that time. Because of it, the Australian government recognised my bachelor's degree, making me eligible to apply for the Subclass 476 Visa.

I only had six months left to apply for the visa as I needed to be in the maximum two-year window from my graduation date. It meant two things. I had to take the International English Language Testing System (IELTS) test immediately as one of the main requirements. Second, I had to resign from my company to pursue this opportunity.

"I will return to Australia," I answered, when asked why I did not want to extend my employment contract at the exit interview with the Human Resources staff.

It took days to gather enough self-esteem to send my resignation letter, as this was my first job since graduation. There was no guarantee I would get the visa to enter Australia. However, making a dream come true requires taking a risk. It includes listening to my inner voice in deciding to fight for my dreams. The last thing I wanted was to be haunted by the guilt of my unfinished dream.

As soon as I became jobless, this inner strength arose within me, knowing I was on the edge. I was in charge of my next step, the IELTS test, which consists of speaking, listening, reading, and writing. My immigration journey depended on the IELTS outcome. As per the visa guidelines, the applicant should have a minimum IELTS score of 6 for each band. My speaking, reading and listening scores were not issues when I took the exam, but my writing mark was 5.5.

My dreams shattered in a heartbeat as I failed to meet the

minimum requirement. It was an outcome I had not expected when I had resigned from work. I'd thought I was more than capable of passing the test, considering I had been using English at work and during the youth exchange program. I'd thought after all the downs, I could finally bounce back. But I still had not hit rock bottom, apparently. I felt like a complete loser who had gone down a spiral, trying to reach everything I could to stop myself from falling.

During my unemployment, I grabbed a lot of casual work as a tour leader and master of ceremonies at various events. The IELTS test costs me around $330, equal to my monthly expenses. Every time I hustled, it would help me to collect the money for my second attempt at the IELTS test.

"Just imagine you are writing something to a friend, so you feel less pressure." I read an article on the online forum to get insight from the people who had obtained a high score in the IELTS writing section.

"Sometimes you think too complicated as an adult. Try to write like a kid telling a simple story and focus sentence by sentence until you complete the whole narration."

I summarised all the writing tips after hours of browsing: *"Basically, I need to have an imaginary friend and write like a child? Okay then!"*

There were moments when I felt frustrated as a non-English speaker. I had to break my mother tongue to pronounce English words properly, and I blocked my brain from thinking in my native language to get used to English grammar. When I took the IELTS test for the second time, it was no longer about whether I could communicate in English. It was a mind game amidst tremendous pressure to meet the visa requirements.

Even 0.5 points would make a huge difference in determining the fate of my visa submission. If only I had been born and grown up in an English-speaking environment, I would have an express ticket on the globalisation journey. English is the key to survival in the immigration escapade.

The light of hope in my dark tunnel finally shone a month after I made a second attempt at the IELTS test. The results showed that all aspects of my exam, including writing, were above 6. One of the main criteria was met, but additional worries awaited me. Besides my English skill, I still needed to pass the character and medical assessment. The police clearance I'd processed in the youth exchange program was enough to satisfy the character check. However, the visa application would most likely be rejected if I had HIV or tuberculosis, as it would be considered a public health funding burden for the Australian government. Every little thing matters as an immigrant. I saw myself as a checklist object, thinking about my language ability and having good character and health. There were too many "what if" scenarios in my mind, speculating the worst possibilities, whereas I was simply too eager for a better life.

The visa journey had been a mental challenge from the first day as I'd organised it myself. Every day was a waiting game, and some days my mind could be my own worst enemy. Three months after I'd lodged the visa application, I was in a car park about to go home when I received an email from the immigration case officer. I let out a big sigh before I opened it. I could have either the worst or the best day of my life in just a couple of seconds. My face was dripping sweat; I swept it away while squinting to read the message line by line until I came across an important statement in the attached files: *"Your visa has been granted."*

I put my bag on the ground and held my phone close to my chest as if I'd just read a love letter. I looked up at the sky and smiled towards the sun. This was the bounce-back moment I had been waiting for.

***

"My visa has been approved, and I will go to Australia for 18 months next week," I said to my parents over dinner in our favourite Sundanese restaurant.

Sometimes I wonder about the things I did to seek my own freedom as a gay man. Moving to Australia with a one-way ticket was my most radical decision ever. I chose to make a living from scratch, find the way back home to myself and leave my family behind. After all, I'd only gotten the visa. That was what worried my parents the most. My mother had cried numerous nights when I was solo backpacking in Southeast Asia for five weeks. She would be more hysterical if she found out I only had an open-plan journey full of uncertainty.

"What about the job and accommodation?" My mum put her spoon and fork on the table.

"Don't worry. I have been in touch with the company where I interned in the youth exchange program. And I will stay with Indonesian friends who study there." I threw sweet lies to give my mum some peace.

"Why do you want to go to Australia? Don't you think gaining work experience in Indonesia first is better?"

"This is a rare opportunity. Not everyone can go to Australia because of the strict visa process." I drank my iced tea while thinking of what to say next. "Worst case, I will come back to Indonesia if I do not like it."

My parents took time to digest their food, as well as my

decision to migrate to Australia. They recognised that I had already made up my mind and that nothing could stop me. Their silence was a sign that they had noticed my white lies about my plans in Australia. I knew I had to hide my fear from them so they would be less distraught. It was about the art of pretending. I smiled at the end of dinner as if I had no qualms. "Let me get the bill."

On my departure day, my parents dropped me off at the bus station in Bandung. They had never imagined that someday they would have to let me go off on this kind of immigration adventure. It was early morning on the weekend, still quiet, and I could tell my mum was worried about me as she occasionally patted my back.

"Do you have enough food and drink?" She made sure I would be comfortable on my two-hour journey to Jakarta.

"You remind me of when I moved from Sulawesi to Java to study at university," my dad reminisced. He thought I was just moving across the sea as he'd done back then. I embodied my dad's adventurous spirit.

It was possible to feel emotional at 5 am if it meant a farewell. My mum could not hide the tears, and my dad hugged me tightly when I was about to get on the bus. It was the warmth of parental love I needed to lighten the weight of my footsteps before I left them.

"It is only for 18 months." I tried to calm them down.

Upon my arrival in Jakarta, I had a send-off dinner with my close friends, who had taken care of me when I was a broke student doing an internship in my final year of university.

"This is a reminder that you will always be the youth ambassador for our country." My friends gave me a sweater with *"Damn, I love Indonesia"* written across the front.

The journey of finding a better version of myself is lifetime work. After having a life-changing experience during the youth exchange program, I knew I did not belong in the same place. I would soon be blooming in nourishing soil. A one-way ticket only stimulated me to dig deeper into who I was supposed to be in a new land.

Getting the visa was only the beginning of my quest. No one could see the future, and I could not even answer to myself how I would survive in a foreign country alone. I just knew I needed this fresh chapter. I wanted to take off all my layers to find my true skin, to cancel all the noise but my inner voice, and to explore the side of me that had never been discovered because of my ingrained preconceptions.

Once more, I was on the plane to see the Australian sky. One of the wishes I had buried inside the box back in Roma, Queensland, had finally come true. Australia had called me again, just a year from the moment I had dug up that earth.

5 THE LIFE FROM ZERO

An economy promo flight took me from Jakarta to Melbourne via Kuala Lumpur. It was 20 hours in the air, and I spent every second of it counting down to the realisation of my dream. If I could have told the pilot to speed up, I would have. My foot was too eager to stomp the Australian terrain to denote my first step.

"Touch down Melbourne!" I posted a selfie on Facebook, welcoming myself in front of Southern Cross Station.

My effort had brought me back to the Land Down Under again. From that moment, every direction I would take was about surviving in a new city by myself. I did not have the privileges of a youth ambassador anymore. There was no chartered transportation and city orientation like the last time I was in Australia. It was just a gloomy day. The combination of the grey sky and drizzling rain was a perfect melancholic setting for a loner immigrant like me.

I picked Melbourne as my first destination because of its art and culture. It was the scene from the tourism video that hooked my attention. There is a girl who rolls large dice twice her size. The dice moves through a hidden laneway capturing trendy coffee shops, art graffiti, and musicians who busk in front of the heritage buildings. The girl is lost at first but ends up discovering surprises as she follows the rolling dice.

Melbourne was where I wanted to build a life from scratch, hoping I could be that girl who rolled the fortune dice, leading me to a better destiny. But the dice had already been played with me, and the game began with a twist.

"Could you please advise me on how to find accommodation in Melbourne and recommend a nice suburb to live in?" I sent a Facebook group message to my youth exchange program friends who lived in Melbourne. *"Let's meet up soon?"* I added.

It was hard to admit that I was in a weak position, a person who did not have much money, a place to live, or close friends in a new country. Being a fresh immigrant carried a lot of pressure because I did not want my friends and family back home to know that I was vulnerable trying to survive. I swallowed my pride when I asked for help; it was just a recommendation on how to find accommodation in Melbourne. And I was already reluctant to do it.

Three of the Australians I knew completely ignored my Facebook message and just disappeared into their routine. Ironically, one of them was the cultural performance coordinator, whom I thought I was close enough to, and she was the one who had eagerly promoted Melbourne to me. We did not even meet for a coffee while I was settling in. I'd thought I had friends, but it turned out the feeling was not mutual.

The person who welcomed me to Australia was a stranger. Through the traveller community website *Couchsurfing*, I found a host who was willing to provide me with a spare couch to stay on. I had nothing to lose and did not have to hide my vulnerability. The man accepted my request to crash for three nights while I was looking for a house share. He had a modern apartment next to St. Kilda Beach. The beautiful sunset of the Melbourne sky could be spotted from the balcony. I pinched myself to make sure what I was seeing was real. That afternoon view guided me to contemplation. My journey was meant to be starting alone without the support of people I knew so I could appreciate the simple blessings. Sleeping on the couch felt like a luxury, looking at St. Kilda Beach felt like a remedy, and talking to my host felt like therapy.

***

Three basic things are needed as an immigrant who starts life from zero to survive in a new country: accommodation, a job, and a circle of friends. The first task was to find a place to live because there was only so long I could stay on the couch. I arranged immediate room inspections after I looked at the online listings. I visited six different places within two days in Melbourne, including accommodations in a dodgy suburb that I had not heard of before.

"Don't you dare to live there! It is a ghetto!" my host warned me after I'd shared my findings.

Having a room inspection is like attending a talent audition. I had to charm the landlords to pick me as a housemate. Most of them were not interested because I did not have a job, and they were afraid I would not be able to pay the rent. Searching for accommodation is also like finding a tribe that shares similarities and backgrounds. I saw an advert stating that a Korean girl was looking for an Asian housemate. The combination of location and rental price made me desperately want the room. It was a brand-new apartment in the central business district area, Southbank, with a rental fee of $125 per week, including all bills. It was below the average rental price for a private room in Melbourne.

I followed Asian etiquette when I met her; I took my shoes off before I went inside, lowered my voice when speaking, threw smiles and nodded my head when listening.

"I do not smoke and drink." I convinced her I was the right person as per her housemate criteria.

"What else do you like?" She leaned against the kitchen wall and intertwined her hands.

"I love the *Full House* TV series so much..." I mentioned a Korean film drama I knew.

She sent a message the following day: *"Can you move into our apartment tomorrow?"*

My charm had paid off. I had found a roof within my first three days in Melbourne. It was an achievement for someone who had started the journey with an open plan.

There is always a catch behind cheap rent. My bedroom was originally a living room space divided into two enclosed areas by a curtain, only 2m x 1.5m. It felt like I was camping inside the apartment with a single mattress that fitted a sleeping bag, a wardrobe rack and a small table. At least I had privacy. Although at night, I could see the nude silhouette of my housemate behind the curtain fabric, an erotic view in a house-share setting.

The apartment had two bedrooms, and two people shared each room. There were six of us from different Asian countries, including Japan, Korea, and Thailand. Some of them had moved to Australia for a working holiday program and study. I had hoped to improve my English when I arrived but ended up teaching them instead. Despite the language barrier, we often shared our cultures through food. I understood why immigrants preferred to stick with their community groups. We all felt the same vulnerability of living in a new country. After spending the whole day lost in translation, we just wanted to return home for a humble dinner that reminded us of family and familiarity. We wished for emotional comfort in a foreign land.

***

First was accommodation, and second was to get an income. It was almost Christmas in 2011 when I arrived in Melbourne. There were plenty of job vacancies, such as waiters, bartenders, and cleaners. Back in Indonesia, university students are supported financially by their parents or by scholarships from the government. It is uncommon to have part-time jobs at cafes or restaurants as they are considered stereotypical jobs for people who do not have access to education. That mindset made me hesitant to apply for a hospitality job in Melbourne. I kept seeing a flash of my memories of working in the office as an engineer in Indonesia. But when I looked at my dwindling savings account, I stopped caring about career prestige. I learned to defeat my ego by dropping off resumes at restaurants and cafes. The reality check was hard, but I had to survive.

"Do you have the food handling certificate?" the restaurant manager asked me.

"Have you got your Responsible Service of Alcohol licence?" said the bar manager.

"Have you done any barista courses previously?" The café manager read my resume.

I had never worked in the hospitality industry before, let alone having formal certification. Meanwhile, my competitors were European backpackers with extensive part-time job experiences gained during university. Finding a hospitality position became as tricky as searching for an office job. It was a competitive market.

I stopped being picky and looked for any job that would give me quick cash. I used the same approach when I found my accommodation, going back to my Asian roots. A Malaysian restaurant in Chinatown captured my attention when I saw the vacancy sign on the front door.

"I worked as a waiter in university back in Indonesia." I made up stories when I handed in my resume.

"I will give you a three-hour trial now if you want." The restaurant owner gave me the menu.

I did not expect to undergo a test to become a waiter, but I had no choice but to fake it. I used my theatre skills to strip off my past identity as an engineer and came out to the floor area as a proud waiter. It felt like a performance every time I greeted the customers, took the orders and served the food. My mum would have been proud that I did not break any glasses or drop any plates during my trial.

"Can you start tomorrow night?" The owner was satisfied with my non-paid three-hour trial shift that afternoon. I started my first job as a full-time waiter in Australia, paying $10 per hour, below the minimum hourly wage.

Finding a job is also about networking. Through a fellow immigrant, I got a recommendation to work in the early morning as a helper at Queen Victoria Market with the incentive of $15 per hour—my hourly rate was more than I'd received as a graduate engineer in Indonesia.

"Do not put that doll over there!" The owner of the toy stall complained when I did not follow her instructions.

My first boss was an old lady from Cambodia. There was no space for improvisation, especially when I displayed the toys on the table. They had to be put in the exact positions they had been in during her thirty years of selling experience. It was a meticulous job, but I gained life perspective every time I listened to her personal stories in quiet moments. She told me about how she'd survived the genocide in 1980. The toys had become a medium to replace her dark stories of the past.

"Sorry if I am too fussy." She patted me on my back. "Because it matters to me. These things symbolise joy." She rearranged the toys while waiting for customers.

My second job at the market was setting up the leather jacket stall. My main task was to install high steel frames at different levels to display various products. It involved tying the string to every corner of the foundations and connecting each of them into columns. I often needed to smash the steel on the floor to shorten and lengthen it, which was noisy and irritating to my ears without ear protection. All the work at this stall required a strong physique. It was even more difficult when my hands were frozen due to Melbourne's cold and windy weather at 6 am. The only thing that could comfort me was the idea of having a hot shower once I returned home as a reward for my physical work at the market.

I was grateful to be earning an income from the beginning of my Australian journey. I worked in the restaurant and market every day while saving money and collecting memories. I learned that the first big leap in settling into a new environment was embracing the new side of me through jobs I'd never thought I would do. It was okay to struggle and not to skip the hard part of my immigration path.

***

For the first couple of weeks in Melbourne, it was enough to merely get through. First was the accommodation, second was the jobs, but the third task was not a linear progression. It took time to build a solid circle of friends because this part I could not fast track. I spoke with my housemates and people at the restaurant, but it was a matter of interaction, not a deep connection. We did not talk about our feelings, just our daily routines. I started to feel lonely, although I was surrounded by people. The migratory grief came to me slowly as I questioned my existence in a new country. I'd left Indonesia to redefine my identity, but it seemed I had lost it in a hustle-bustle metropolitan city. Online dating became my getaway, and I had several dates during my days off to abate the loneliness.

"Do you want to come over to my place?" I got picked up at the gay bar with guy number one.

"You have nice lips." I kissed guy number two on a rainy night.

"Cheers to us!" I drank champagne at the park with guy number three.

"Have you been to this area before?" Guy number four drove me around town in an open-top car.

The dates did not progress further because of the complication of my work roster. However, it was alluring to have those infatuations. I needed intimacy and connection with someone to remind me that I was not just an immigrant trying to survive in a new place. I did not want to become anonymous, an invisible person in a city where people did not notice my presence. I was more than just a number in Australia's immigration statistics. I wanted to be part of someone's life.

I was an immigrant who had started life from zero. Despite all the hardships, I was able to find accommodation, jobs and new friends. But there was more to it. Life from zero taught me to engage with myself twenty-four hours every day. I had no option except to self-motivate, face the daily challenges, and appreciate all my efforts to survive.

My loneliness as a new immigrant gave me a different perspective. I was aware of my senses because I shared all my memories with myself. I found comfort when I sat next to the window on the tram. It became more than ordinary public transportation but a recollection shelter for me. It contained a memory of when I'd carried my luggage to St. Kilda after arriving at Southern Cross Station. I found comfort when I walked down the road on which every footstep was memorable. Strolling around the city contained a memory of searching for hospitality jobs. I found comfort in the strangers who became my acquaintances, a dream and hope that became a reality, a hard time that made me evolve, and all the melodies from the buskers that became the soundtrack of my day. It started from zero, and every inch of progress I made was worth so much.

I kept rolling my fortune dice every day between working and meeting people. Sometimes I was lost, and another day I was found. Melbourne has its own game to make people stay and leave.

6 THE FESTIVAL

The learning curve of surviving in Melbourne had been an exponential ride for the first two months. What I needed was a break at the end of the year to find momentum and settle my roller-coaster of emotions. It was also the time to reflect on my journey so far. I wanted to make a fresh start in the new year and see the progress of my Australian dream within the annual timeline.

ConFest appeared to me when I craved a life intermission. It was an alternative festival held in a rural area between the Victoria and New South Wales border. The highlight mentioned on the internet was there would be a full moon drum party on New Year's Eve. Dancing under the moonlight was enough to excite me. The universe agreed with my plan and granted me a rideshare to get to the festival through a Facebook event page.

"Ready to go?" An Australian guy and a backpacker girl from the Netherlands picked me up.

I sat in the back seat, a third wheel watching the guy trying to make a move on her.

"We can set up our tents next to each other." He shifted his body towards the backpacker girl.

"Let's see how it goes." She kept looking out the left side

window, avoiding eye contact.

"Do you mind if I nap?" she asked the Australian guy. "I'm tired from working last night." The backpacker girl curled up on the front passenger seat, leaning towards the door.

"So, have you been to ConFest before?" The Australian guy looked at me through the rear-view mirror.

"Pardon?" I leaned forward, struggling to understand his strong accent.

"Oh, right," was my default reply whenever he said something I did not comprehend.

"Hahaha!" I faked a laugh every time he made a joke, even though I did not get the content.

The Australian guy had been kind to offer me a ride. The least I could do was to keep him company through the conversation. But I was ashamed I could not connect due to his thick accent. In the end, I followed the backpacker girl's trick, pretending to fall asleep until we arrived at the festival in the vast bushland. Without air conditioning in the car, sweat was dripping off my face as we were immediately battling with the 30-degree temperature. I opened the window, hoping to get some fresh air. But the surrounding area was dry, and the dirt from the spinning tires dominated my view.

"Welcome to ConFest, guys!" A topless man wearing a purple tutu and a curly red wig greeted us at the gate.

"Here you go." I gave him $80 for the ticket fee.

"Are you a first-timer?" He handed out the festival guidebook.

We entered one week of a new world in the Australian outback as we passed the entrance. After setting up our tents, the three of us decided to explore the festival separately. At first, I was nervous about what I would do if I wandered around alone. But I remembered the festival guidebook intro: *"We are a fun-loving and tolerant community."*

There was a river five minutes' walk from my tent, a good spot to enjoy the sunset. Everything became clearer as I approached; it was a clothing-optional area. People of various ages, including kids, gathered naked. I tried not to stare at them and kept looking at the ground. When I took my shirt off, I felt a sense of rebellion; my religion and culture prohibited nudity. My mind was spinning, and I worried about stripping off my underwear in public for the first time, wondering how people would react when they saw my genitalia. I sat down for a while looking at the river, battling with my thoughts.

My parents had taught me that nudity was only appropriate during showers and sex. They might have thought I was at an orgy party if they knew where I was. But that was the preconception I'd had before arriving at the festival. Though the people were nude, they talked respectfully to each other and even managed to play beach volleyball together. I decided to remove my underwear, knowing it was a safe space in which to be naked. Nonetheless, I still ran as fast as I could while covering my penis with my hands before jumping into the river, making it more obvious that I was shy. The water soon relaxed me, and I was comfortable with my nudity, like a newborn baby.

The first time I stripped off all my clothes in public was the moment I fully accepted myself in a new country. It was not because I wanted to be a hippy but because I liked letting go of my prejudice about nudity and embracing my body instead. I learned quickly to set my penis free and was not hesitant to gather with people near the bonfire by the river.

"It is such a beautiful sunset, isn't it?" I stood one foot apart from a man with thick chest hair.

"I can't wait to attend the workshop." He rubbed his hands to get some heat.

Having a conversation while naked turned out to be very liberating. The world did not end when I was in the nude.

The festival was a non-profit volunteer-run event focusing on bringing a range of people and alternative cultures together while exploring a communal experience. During the day, anyone could share their talents, skills, and ideas by hosting independent workshops in a designated tepee. The topics varied from a spontaneous choir, dancing, philosophical discussions, tai chi, body contact, laughter yoga, tantra massage, fire twirling, and circus skills to mantra chanting. With one rule: monetary payment during the workshop was neither accepted nor made.

"Welcome to the kissing class!" This was one of my favourite activities at ConFest.

"I am going to start with basic greetings from different cultures," said the mentor in front of the audience. "We will start with handshaking, hugging, and then kissing cheek to cheek." He gave a quick demonstration to his female assistant.

"Anyone know the Hongi greeting from the Maori tribe?" He touched his forehead and nose tip against his assistant's face while maintaining eye contact. "If you are ready, practise those greetings in this circle."

The mentor went on to talk about the next activity, the three-second lip-kissing rule.

"It is about a gentle feeling, okay?" He showed how to do it with a male volunteer and raised his voice. "No tongue! Anyone uncomfortable doing it can stay out of this circle."

I decided to join the three-second kissing exercise to push my boundaries further than being naked at the river. I aimed for good-looking guys, but I ended up kissing some girls.

"As we approach the last exercise, I will split the group in half." The mentor waved his hand at the crowd as if cutting a cake. "The first group will be blindfolded, while the rest will give a kiss to part of their body. Got it?"

I could not help giggling as I felt ticklish when some people kissed behind my ear, my sensitive spot. I enjoyed the workshop because the art of kissing had finally broken down the language barrier between the local people and me. No talking, just kissing.

***

Between the workshop tents and the river area, I often bumped into a bearded guy with a well-built body and green eyes. I referred to him as the man with a full back tattoo. I'd first noticed him at the kissing workshop, though we did not kiss each other. I was unsure about his sexual orientation until I spotted him sitting in the corner of the LGBTQIA+ gathering. We finally exchanged our first hello when we were covered in mud naked while doing a zombie walk activity.

"Do you do massage?" He approached me at the chill-out tent next to the river after we'd cleaned the mud from our bodies.

Since our first encounter, I'd written everything about him in my diary: the workshop we attended together, how he smiled, how he talked, and the outfit he wore. Each day I had something new about him to adore, and I became his admirer.

"I will be waiting at the information centre at a quarter to twelve." I gave a note to him on New Year's Eve. *"Will you be my midnight kiss?"*

The Festival

My desire for him had escalated due to the full moon's energy. But there was no sign of him when I arrived at the meeting point. As we approached the new year countdown, people kept rushing towards the drum circle. One, five, and ten minutes passed without his presence. My inner voice told me to cancel the idea of having a midnight kiss with him. I reminded myself that dancing under the moonlight was the reason I'd attended the festival. It was not about a fairy-tale love scene.

The drum rhythm took me to the centre of the dance floor. I was a few metres from the bonfire, surrounded by strangers. It was loud with percussion music, and my brain cells brought back the memory of the New Year's Eve kiss I had had with my counterpart a year ago. The full moon spirit took me high above to a nostalgic dimension. It left me lonely not to have someone to hold in the middle of the crowd.

"Happy new year!" People started to hug each other when the new year finally came.

I closed my eyes and began to express my void emotion through spontaneous tribal acapella, accompanied by the drum circle's vibrancy. Music never failed me, I thought. I sang my heart out to the universe until someone behind me tapped my shoulder.

"Sorry I couldn't see you before midnight as I was with friends," said the man with the full back tattoo.

"That's all right, man." I patted back.

"So, about the kiss?" He stepped forward.

"Well, be my guest." I held both his hands.

Midnight had already passed, but the full moon above the dark sky did not miss witnessing the two men who finally kissed. It was not sensual, more of the three-second gentle kiss on the lips—a friendly touch for a hopeless romantic like me. I could not have asked for a better serotonin dose that night. Some people danced under the moonlight, and some people kissed. I had both to mark my fortune on the new year's journey.

The next day, the man with the full back tattoo was at the entrance gate doing a volunteer shift. He farewelled the punters who were about to leave the festival. I opened the car window when I passed the gate and gave my diary to him. It was a goodbye present to my outback infatuation since I would never see him again. I remember the farewell message I wrote:

"I just wish that we spoke the same language.

I wish I could describe the magical feeling I felt whenever I saw you unexpectedly in the workshops.

I wish that I could speak my emotions directly from my mouth.

A message on a piece of paper tastes cold, like frozen food.

You cannot see my hand shaking as I write this to you.

Remember, you are part of my festival memories.

And I thank you for being you.

P.S. Keep dancing under the moonlight. That's where you can find me."

***

My casual jobs at the restaurant and Queen Victoria Market were waiting when I got back to Melbourne. It lasted only a few weeks as some people at ConFest had suggested that I go to Tasmania for Rainbow Gathering. I worked long hours and saved a lot of money in exchange for booking the cheapest economy ticket to Tasmania.

Through a backpacker website, I found travel-mates from Germany and Italy to join a two-week road trip. We followed the campsite guidebook to experience the Tasmanian outback lifestyle, as it is illegal to camp in random areas. Back in Indonesia, camping meant skipping the shower for days and digging holes to hide my faeces. But here, I was spoiled with public toilets, showers and even a barbecue area. Every night we sat outdoors to inspire and be inspired. Under the southern hemisphere's stars, we shared our life journeys and dreams in Australia.

"Do you want to attend a hippy festival called Rainbow Gathering in the Cradle Mountain National Park?" I talked to my travel-mates while watching the fire pit.

"Yeah! I want to camp in the forest." The Italian guy who drove the van agreed with my itinerary.

Rainbow Gathering was hidden somewhere in Cradle Mountain. We had to follow the clues written on the Facebook group's page and kept driving on the road until we found a flag tied to a tree. Each hint brought us closer to the river area. After hours of driving, a large, colourful hand-crafted banner greeted us at the campsite entrance. It read, *"Welcome Home."*

Rainbow Gathering was not a festival full of activities like ConFest. It was a slowdown moment to connect with nature, together with people who referred to one another as brother and sister. The communal events were organised voluntarily, with no hierarchy or leader. Nobody was allowed to use electronic devices. It was a hippy world where I started my morning by bathing in the cold Tasmanian river and warming up naked by the sacred fire. In the middle of the forest, people found their own freedom.

"Every little cell in my body is happy. Every little cell in my body is happy and well." The crowd sang a gratitude song.

People gathered around the sacred fire in a circle formation for every lunch and dinner. We always sang a couple of hippy songs before the volunteers served food.

"Coin donation, please." The kitchen team would approach us once we had finished eating, so they could buy the next meal.

Sometimes people shared their personal stories with the crowd, delivering peace and love messages at the end of the food circle. However, I always returned to the campervan to hang out with my travel-mates. We often discussed our daily experiences of becoming full-time hippies at Rainbow Gathering.

"We cannot force ourselves to live in harmony all the time," said my German travel-mate.

"I like to express anger and silly arguments," I replied.

"We need to earn money to survive in Australia. We cannot just live for today and not think about tomorrow," the Italian guy added.

It lasted only three days before we decided to leave Rainbow Gathering and return to civilisation. Hobart was my final destination on the road trip while they continued to explore West Tasmania. I could not have asked for better companions to make my adventure unforgettable. In the farewell moment, I questioned when I would see them again. It is a traveller's fate to keep wandering because everyone has a quest to discover. My encounter with them helped me to unfold a new life chapter. But in the end, I am the one who makes sense of the stories.

"See you again someday, somewhere." I gave my travel-mates a big hug.

Hobart welcomed me for some long-overdue closure. It was a special holiday destination for my counterpart. I walked around the city while having a flashback about him, a monologue from the past. My perspective had changed after attending the recent festivals. I believed there was always a good side of my counterpart as an individual. He could be a best friend to some people, the best son to his parents, or the best lover to his partner. But when I met him back then, we shared a version of ourselves that we never discovered before. For my part, I realised I had been trapped by my own expectations. I sometimes romanticised that Andrew was my boyfriend. It would be nice to tell the story of how we met in the youth exchange program. It would be romantic to say we kissed on New Year's Eve. It would be special to have a same-sex love story between two countries, Indonesia and Australia. All this time, I'd been trying hard to create perfect tales between us, although I knew he was not compatible with me. I liked having romantic stories to the point that I forced myself to fit into his mould. When I met him, I tried to like someone with my gentle heart, even if it was hurt, or even if it was not meant to be. It was because I wanted to see how deep I could pour my heart out in the name of romance.

    I did my part to prove I was strong enough to endure the painful feelings. I cherished myself for finally making my way to Hobart, and marked my presence in his special place as part of my healing process. Some people seek closure by throwing away photos or cutting off communication. But I set foot in his favourite spot to finally move on.

7 THE WEST COAST

The biggest migration survival skill is knowing when to stay and to leave. That was what I learned about Melbourne after I returned from Tasmania. It was time to depart.

Living in a vibrant city and fighting with reality had left me with countless nights of contemplation. My Melbourne experiences were stuck between the restaurant and the market bubbles. The high-rise building along the Yarra River had been a loyal spectator to my struggle whenever I went back and forth working long hours as a waiter and a helper. I was exhausted, and I'd lost weight. I asked myself, *"Is this the kind of lifestyle I wanted to pursue when I moved from Indonesia?"*

I did not want to give up my career as an engineer yet. A high-skilled job could allow me to stay in Australia once my 18-month visa expired. While I'd found a way back to Australia through my degree, it was not enough to make Melbourne home. The city was not for an oil and gas worker like me. Forget about getting an interview; I stumbled just to find a job vacancy related to my niche field in ocean engineering. Every time I sent unsolicited applications, I begged the universe for at least one company to be kind enough to notice me. I was ready to climb up from the very bottom of the career ladder by doing an unpaid internship. Even so, no corporation wanted to share their spare seat with me, not a single chair amongst hundreds of offices in Melbourne.

It was heart-wrenching to pack up all my belongings for a departure. It meant crushing and shredding my Melbourne wish list. I dreamed of enjoying dinner in a fancy restaurant along the Yarra River every time I passed the Southbank area. I dreamed of watching theatre performances whenever I walked around the Arts Centre. I dreamed of going shopping and hanging out at a chic bar every time I went to a funky suburb like Brunswick or Fitzroy. I gave up those wishes as I did not have enough currency to afford those Melbourne enchantments.

Diverted from my original migration plan, settling in Melbourne, was like driving a car without navigation. I sought any sign along the journey that would lead me back to the right track. People indicated the next clue, and it all pointed to the west coast. They whispered about the mining boom success stories. A cleaner or a driver could earn much more than white-collar office employees. The potential income and job opportunities lured me. I booked a flight to a place that was not on my radar at all: Perth, Western Australia. There were uncertainties ahead of me. But searching for new possibilities was part of survival. It is the art of the migration journey.

***

I stood on Perth's ground, less of a hustle-and-bustle city and warmer than Melbourne. It gave me space to breathe and debrief until my limited savings reminded me that I could not sit and relax. Every day became a money battle. I stayed in a cheap backpacker hostel where the room was old and dirty, convenient for cockroaches to roam around the floor. The room could not be locked because the door was rotten. The only option was to carry my important stuff wherever I went. The first night I lay on the bottom bunk bed, I questioned myself: *"What am I doing here?"*

I gave myself three days to find a house share so I could stop killing the cockroaches at the hostel. I did a similar exercise to what I'd done in Melbourne, selling my best impression to the landlord in the name of room hunting. I would look them in the eyes and rely on their mercy to consider me as a prospective tenant. On the second day of room viewings, I got accepted to stay in a private bedroom for $150 per week, including all bills. Unlike my room in Melbourne, which was separated by the curtain, this time I had a wall made of brick. Before sleeping on the first night, I told myself, *"Finally!"*

My house share was an hour's commute from the city centre, bus and train combined. Thornlie was a suburb where my bike got stolen three times from the garage and train stations. The sound of a police siren was routine on weekend nights, like when they raided my neighbour as part of a drug-dealing investigation. I also could not forget when a group of teenagers spat at me from a bridge as I cycled home from the train station. I grabbed the handlebars so hard that my hands burned, and used my anger to cycle as fast as I could. I wanted to fight back, but I was too afraid they would attack me. That afternoon, I saw myself as an immigrant who had signed up for a tough life in a rough neighbourhood.

The bright side about moving to Perth was a reunion with my fellow AIYEP participants. The first was with Kiki, an Indonesian delegate from South Sulawesi province who had shared a host family with me in Brisbane. She had moved to Perth following a year in a teaching assistant program for the

Indonesian language subject at a primary school. There was only excitement when we reunited in front of a green, $1 million, 6.5 metre-high cactus sculpture. A familiar person from the past in a new city at last. We did not need to discover and adjust to each other.

"Have you learnt how to cook rice without burning it?" She laughed at me.

"Don't worry. There are a few Indonesian restaurants here," I smiled.

The second reunion was with Jenny, an AIYEP delegate from Adelaide, who was the Community Development leader back then. We went for dinner when she visited Perth for a business trip with her law firm. She lifted my spirits with a handful of advice and motivation for my job hunting. We cheered over beers while we reminisced about our youth exchange program memories.

"Don't worry! I have a gay brother who lives in the Philippines with his boyfriend." She hugged me when I came out to her.

"You know what shocks me about my counterpart?" I paused for a couple of seconds, gathering the words. "I heard that he's married to a woman now."

"I was surprised too when I saw their wedding pictures on Facebook." Her jaw dropped.

There was not much interaction between Jenny and me during the youth exchange program. But I felt a connection with her at our dinner reunion. She proved more genuine than the Australian delegates who had encouraged me to move to Melbourne but had disappeared when I was finally there. Sometimes it only takes a small gesture to change the whole friendship narrative.

James became the third person I had a reunion with; he had also been in charge of the AIYEP Community Development project. Like Jenny, I'd rarely hung out with him during the youth exchange program. However, he was kind-hearted, showing Kiki and me the outback life in Western Australia.

"Make sure you don't catch the baby crabs!" James shouted when we went crabbing in Mandurah, an hour's drive from Perth city centre.

"Just use this stick to measure them?" I asked James, as it was my first-time crabbing.

On another occasion, James took me camping in his van.

"It's like snow in the desert!" I was amazed to see vast white sands in the middle of dry habitation at Lancelin Sand Dunes.

"This is stunning!" I saw rocks coming from the ground when we drove around The Pinnacles, a sacred place for Aboriginal tribes.

These unbeaten adventures opened my eyes to the west coast beauty and helped me forget the job-hunting stress for a while. I had not felt rich as a new immigrant since arriving in Perth. Not until I encountered the episode of AIYEP reunion and the magic of the Western Australian landscape, which is so diverse, wild and unique.

***

My circumstances remained the same for my first month in Perth: still jobless. I did not tell anyone that deep down, I was struggling to stay above water. My family and friends back in Indonesia only knew of my so-called happy life based solely on a glimpse of social media impressions. As an Indonesian, stepping foot overseas was already considered an achievement. To spot me smiling with a background of Perth city centre was a sign of opulence. Migration was more about living in a city with a clean environment, fewer traffic jams and less pollution. At my worst, it was mostly about survival mode. Behind the social media façade, I worried about meeting my basic needs to eat and stay under a roof once my savings dried out.

There were days I wished someone could save me from the hardships of living in Australia. When I met up with some of the Indonesians who lived in Perth, I realised I was in a different situation to them. I wished I had moved to Australia with a job offer like Kiki. I wished my parents could support me financially, like Budi, who studied at Curtin University. I wished I had found a boyfriend who wanted to marry me like Andi, whose husband provided a house and daily expenditure after they'd met in Bali. I knew we all had struggles that we could not see. But I was desperate; I liked the whole idea of waiting for a saviour to come into my life.

The negative energy took me to a deep, dark place where I could not see the light. At my most hopeless, living in Indonesia with a job guarantee and support from family and friends seemed a better option than living in a developed country with nothing. All I could think of when I looked in the mirror was, *"Who is going to save me now?"*

When life gets tough, sometimes the version of ourselves in the past is the only one who can be a cheerleader in our present. It was a constant effort to keep reminding myself of why I'd wanted to move to Australia in the first place, about the myriad of restless nights in which I'd had to make peace with my sexual orientation, and who I was as a Pink Ranger. I tried to remember how I'd survived backpacking through Southeast Asia alone. I pictured the wishes I'd buried one foot underneath outback soil in Roma, Queensland. I revisited the photos and videos I'd taken since arriving in Australia, especially the recent road trip to Tasmania, knowing I'd met incredible people along the way. My inner voice convinced me that I had always been a saviour to myself. I am the one in charge of my destiny.

"How have you been?" Andrea, my Italian travel-mate from the Tasmanian trip, called me.

"I am still adjusting. How about yourself?" I replied.

"Hmmm, not good." He paused.

"What happened?" I raised my voice.

"You would not believe this. David passed away." He referred to our German travel-mate, who had shared the van and tent with us during the road trip in Tasmania. "He continued his adventure to Queensland to visit the waterfall with other backpackers. It was a rainy day when they climbed the rocks. Unfortunately, he slipped and lost his balance at the edge of the waterfall, and he died on the spot," he sobbed.

Only a week before receiving the tragic news, I'd posted video footage about our Tasmania road trip to lift my mood during my desperate time in Perth. I could not help but burst into tears when I heard David was gone too soon—at only 24 years old.

My memories of the silly things we'd done together were still vivid. We used to play cards to decide who would refill the water for dishwashing and carry it from the river to the campervan. We used to share delicious food in the middle of the cold night. He was a witty boy who'd splashed a bucket of water on me when I'd fallen asleep in the hammock on a hot day. He'd engraved the peace symbol into a piece of wood to replicate my hippy necklace, so we had matching memories. I remember when he'd told me of his aspiration: "I want to go back to Germany to continue my master's degree and also visit Indonesia soon!"

Andrea and I got in touch with David's family after the tragedy, and his parents gathered photos of him from our trip as last recollections. Words in my eulogy could not summarise the intensity of our connection in Tasmania.

"David was a young man with big dreams. He reminded me that life was too short not to explore off the beaten tracks and unfamiliar places. He lived his life to the fullest. Even on his last day, he was on the top of his quest and full of adrenaline."

His spirit inspired me to get through uncertainties and enjoy the wild young adventure. I am alive, and I should keep my excitement in life going. I made a promise to his soul that I would push my limits. Every time I felt like I wanted to give up, I would have one last try to continue his legacy. His memories fuelled me to bounce back from the adversity during my unemployment period in Perth. On the west coast, I had my epiphany.

8 THE JOB

People call it luck, which is a way of turning the human predicament into basic logic. But some luck is complex and built from tenacity. It looks ugly, impossible, and frightening. I was up against all the odds in my job search; fresh graduate, new immigrant, and non-English speaker with a limited working visa. The only thing that motivated me to keep going was the unknown. It gave me the excitement to enjoy the game.

Since receiving countless automatic rejection emails or worse, not hearing from the company at all, my job searching approach had become more radical. I used a gay dating website to look for an engineering job. I thought if someone liked me enough, they would not hesitate to help me. The result was gloomy at the start. Those strangers did not bother with my profile description and went directly for a sex date proposal. However, it only took one anonymous message to restore my hope.

"*I could help you,*" read the text in the inbox.

The offer came from a discreet gay man without a profile photo. It was not a concern as my intention was not for a hook-up. I went to his place for a bigger mission, discussing my resume and potential job information.

"Come on in." A heavy six-foot-tall mature man opened the door.

I sat down next to him in the living room. "Can I have a glass of water, please?"

"I could definitely assist you with this job search." He handed me the glass.

To say that I was sceptical about his background was an understatement. He clearly sensed my doubt and showed me a private library where he stored academic books related to oil and gas.

"Keep this." The man gave me his business card.

My eyes got hooked on the job title; he was one of the project directors in a multinational mining company. I utilised our evening as a spontaneous coaching session where I asked about his career path for hours.

"I will forward your resume to the Human Resources and Engineering Departments. I will introduce you as my colleague's son." He winked.

My mind flew high, lightening the burden. I was euphoric when I received an interview invitation by email from the Human Resources staff a few days later. It had taken me five months since arriving in Australia to finally secure my first job interview. An online dating website had allowed me to take the next step in my professional career. It was an approach I had not thought would work until I was hopeless.

Golden opportunities do not come often. I brought three A3-size posters with me on the day of my first job interview. They captured the visual information about my resume, Ocean Engineering syllabus, and company profile. I wanted to steal the interviewer's attention while explaining my skills and background. They had allocated time to meet me, and it was my turn to serve them with my enthusiasm.

"Oh, wow!" The engineering manager pointed at the posters.

My first interview was an hour of exerting effort, and I felt so close to my goal. Every second, I prayed for my English to be smooth coming out of my mouth. One answer at a time.

"It is good to hear about your experience. You seem to be a suitable candidate for our graduate program that runs every year." The engineering manager paused the conversation while she grabbed something from her folder. "Unfortunately, we started the new cohorts a couple of months ago." She passed me the graduate program booklet. "I suggest waiting until the next graduate engineer intake opens next year."

It was the right opportunity, but not at the right time. My 18-month visa clock had been ticking for five months, and I could not afford to wait for another year. The project director I'd met online could not help me to secure the job instantly. I was just a fresh graduate with little work experience, after all.

Despite the outcome, I left the company building with my chin up. The whole experience taught me a valuable lesson on how to get the interview opportunity: it is not always about how impressive my resume is, but who I sleep with.

***

My desperation had reached its peak. The next strategy of my job searching was to make door-to-door applications by showing up at office buildings and hoping I could arrange a spontaneous interview. It sounded like a heroic approach at the beginning. But my hands and feet often shook when I stood before the skyscrapers. It involved a ritual where I wasted fifteen minutes of my life gathering my confidence before taking the first step inside.

Overcoming the panic was just an initial hurdle. Sometimes

The Job

I could not even access the lift as it required a guest card to pass the security gate. The receptionist played a vital role in every spontaneous visit, and they became the executor of my door-to-door job application outcome.

"You can apply on the website…" Many receptionists indicated a soft rejection.

Showing up at office buildings was not just a sign of despair. I genuinely wanted to show my eagerness and personality, more than a two-dimensional version of me that was captured in a piece of resume. Only a few people could vibe with my intention. One of the receptionists was moved by my situation after I had made countless attempts. She quickly called the Human Resources Department when I showed up in front of her.

"Just wait there." She pointed to the chair beside her desk.

I could not hide my smile, knowing I might get my first spontaneous interview. The company I'd visited had a great reputation worldwide. Back in Indonesia, only fresh graduate students with a cum laude title got accepted to work with them.

"I'm Andy. Nice to meet you." The Human Resources staff member greeted me in the lobby.

"Thank you for your time." I gave my resume to him.

He read it in silence. I had speculations about his stillness; maybe he'd spotted grammatical errors, or my skills were not good enough.

"I am going to arrange an interview in the upcoming days. Please send your resume to my email." He handed me a business card.

There had not been any better day than when I finally scored a job interview opportunity due to an impromptu visit. Moving to Perth had indicated a good omen so far. I kept rolling my luck until the interview day and brought three A3-size posters for the second time—my signature move.

"What did you do exactly during your internship with British Petroleum?" A bald man pointed out a chart on my poster.

"Any experience with designing breakwaters or onshore jetties?" Another senior engineer jumped onto the interrogation bandwagon.

Layer by layer, the interviewers peeled back the presentation material I'd brought. Some questions were challenging because they focused on coastal engineering instead of offshore structures, which was my thesis topic.

The recruitment process was followed by an online aptitude test a few days later. There were fifty questions over twenty minutes. The pressure of getting the job was more difficult to handle than the assessment itself. My mind raced between what I saw on the screen and what my brain was thinking. It left me with a pile of doubts as the time ticked down from minutes to seconds. I barely answered half of the test.

"We regret to inform you that your application was unsuccessful…" I read the first sentence of an email sent by the company a week later. The opening line was already too sharp for my heart. It felt like it had been cut by a knife. I knew I'd done my best, but the disappointment was there, hanging five centimetres before my eyes. I'd been so close to getting employed. It would have been a perfect story for the world to know that a boy had shown up spontaneously at the office building and got his dream job. Sadly, it was just an almost-success story for me.

***

Two months of job searching in Perth had passed by. Working on a mining site as a labourer awaited me as the last option.

The Job

My goal shifted from settling in Australia to earning as much money as possible. In my mind, I could use the funds to pursue a master's degree or set up a business if I had to go back to Indonesia. At least I'd tried. The southern cross stars knew I had given all I had.

There was one engineering consultancy left on my list that I was yet to visit. They had already sent me a rejection email back in Melbourne. But when I rechecked the website, there were another three affiliated businesses under their brand. I thought it would be different if I showed up in person and tested my luck with their sister company.

"Good afternoon." I smiled at the receptionist in the lobby. "I was wondering if I could drop my resume here in case of a vacant position?"

"Okay, just leave it to me," she replied quickly.

I left the building, suspecting my resume would end up in the rubbish bin. That was it, the moment when I committed to look for labourer jobs on the mining site. The next day, however, I received an acknowledgement email from the engineering manager about my application.

"Are you available for an interview sometime next week?"

This was my final attempt to perform all out. I prepared three different A3-size posters for the third time. It was a weapon for my ultimate battle against two interviewees. First was the Scottish engineering manager, and second was the French senior engineer.

"So, Ozak, could you please introduce yourself?" said the manager.

I had already anticipated the question. "I've actually brought these posters as my presentation material. Do you mind?"

"I have never interviewed anyone like this before. Please, go ahead." The manager gave me a signal.

I explained my engineering work experience in flowchart format. It was colourful enough to get attention, not to mention the size of the poster.

"I would say you have good technical internship experience. Although your first working experience after graduation was unrelated to technical work. It was more project management."

I continued with the second poster, explaining the Ocean Engineering syllabus and the scores I got from the main study subjects related to offshore engineering.

"The curriculum is similar to the one I studied back in France, like Structural Dynamics, Offshore Structures Design, Water Wave Mechanics, and Hydrodynamic subjects," said the senior engineer. "Reading your academic transcript reminds me of my university life."

I moved on to the last poster and explained the projects I was interested in within the company.

"To be honest, not many people knew about our company's capabilities since we are doing niche work focusing on flexible riser technology. I appreciate that you have researched what we do," the manager commented.

He gave back my three posters. "Now, I also want to hear about your technical engineering knowledge. Could you please explain the calculation theory used for your thesis project?"

My intuition was right; they would ask about my thesis as I had applied for a reputable engineering consultancy job. Reviewing the theoretical part was one of the preparations I had done the night before. I wrote down the formula of the hydrodynamic equation used in the offshore platform application. I put the pen down, hoping it was the first and last technical question he would ask.

"The second question is about basic mechanical engineering. I am going to draw a beam with force. Could you draw what the load distribution would look like?" He gave me a piece of blank paper.

My worst interview nightmare had come true. I wanted to cry out loud because the question was a subject I'd learned in my second year of university. I grabbed the pen, and I could feel my palm sweating. My brain cells tried to remember the answer from my dusty memories. In silence, I could hear my inner voice, *"Use your logic!"*

Everything I did in that time dimension felt like it was moving in slow motion. I drew the distribution load as if walking on a tightrope, cautious from the beginning until the end. It was my instinct that helped me wrap up the answer.

"How do you still remember that? Good job!" The manager shook my hand. "I think we've got everything we need here. As the last step, we will do a reference check before we make the final decision."

A week had gone by since the interview. It was 4 pm when I received a phone call from an unrecognised number, and I was in my room when I answered it.

"It is me, Simon, who interviewed you last week. How are you going, Ozak?"

"Hi, Simon! I am very well, thank you." I jumped from my bed and held my phone closer to my ear.

"What did you think about your interview with us?" His Scottish accent swamped my listening.

"It was a nice experience. I became more interested in the

company after I visited the office." I scratched my leg as I was talking, nervous. I could not tell if his question was a good or bad sign.

"That is good to hear! The feeling is mutual. We would like to have you work with us. We will send you a job contract, and you can let us know what you think."

The adrenaline rushed through my veins, increasing my blood flow and heartbeat. I could not hold in the excitement after I hung up the phone and screamed at the top of my lungs in my room until I could hear my own echo. My whole body trembled as I processed the information I had just received. My face turned red, and tears came from my eyes within seconds. I dropped my phone and lay on the floor, hugging myself tightly. I allowed myself a moment of self-appreciation. It did not matter if I looked messy with my runny nose, or if I was wailing until I ran out of breath. Those afternoon cries were my restoration from the struggles of the past five months. There were no scars, but piles of frightening moments from standing alone in the middle of a metropolis to exchanging my hopelessness for a job opportunity. And I had done it, beating all the odds and creating my own luck.

My housemate took me to the Anzac Day dawn service the next morning. I stood in the crowd, feeling the meaning of sacrifice as I followed the commemoration ceremony in total silence. Once it had finished, we walked to the hill to welcome the sunrise. It was an unforgettable panorama; everything around me was beautiful in solitude. I took a long breath while looking at the dark sky slowly turning to gold. Beneath the horizon, there was hope about my future that would be as bright as the sunrise before my eyes.

The Job

Another dream I'd buried under the Australian outback soil had come true. It had arrived when I was on the edge of despair, saving me from giving up. And for the first time, I felt that Australia had finally opened its door to me. The job offer had moulded my immigration journey into one that would be filled with vivacious stories.

9 THE WEDDING

It was my big moment. I woke up half an hour before the 6 am alarm, excited to have a whole new adventure on my first day at work. I'd even ironed my shirt twice just to make sure I looked sharp. Every step I took towards the train station felt like I was going to kindergarten. Fun times lay ahead of me. I was ready to play the adult game again, joining the feisty rush-hour commute.

"Good morning!" I waved to the receptionist when I arrived at the lobby. She was the one who had forwarded my resume to the engineering manager, and I thanked her for that.

The lift took me to the fourth floor, and I could not stop practising my best smile in front of the mirror. I waited for the door to open as if I was an actor waiting for the theatre curtain to rise, wondering who was in the audience.

"Hi, Ozak! Good to see you again!" My engineering manager welcomed me in the hallway.

I'd made it. It felt magical when I finally sat at my desk to see my name badge attached to the cubicle wall: Arozak Salam. The day could not get any better when my director invited me to have lunch with him. He wanted to get to know me, like a date, which rarely happens back in Indonesia as the workplace environment is hierarchical. We talked about world news over sandwiches and coffee. It was also my opportunity to ask him about his professional background and show my enthusiasm as a new employee.

"Let me get the bill." I made a move to be polite, although he was the one who paid.

At the end of the first week, my boss threw welcome drinks for me at the Irish pub across from the office. It was my introduction to alcohol. Not only did I want to mingle with my colleagues, but also I could not refuse free stuff, given the company covered the drinks. They quickly noticed my face turned red just from a glass of chardonnay. It was apparent that I could not compete in the drinking game against my Irish, Scottish and Australian co-workers.

My life excitement did not stop with my new routine at work. Just a few days after I got the job, my sister in Indonesia shared the big news, "I'm getting married in November!"

I'd started a new career at the perfect time, six months before my sister's wedding. Her invitation gave me additional motivation to perform well at work so I could pass my probation. Every day I learned something new, and every month I saved money to buy a plane ticket and fund a week-long trip to Indonesia. I wanted to bring a success story when I visited my family. It is an immigrant's dream to leave their loved ones without them worrying and make them proud when coming back home. It is an immigrant's dignity to keep what happened between leaving and returning to themselves because all the sacrifices and struggles are just the price that must be paid.

***

Many things had happened since I'd left my hometown, Bandung. When I returned, I wondered whether what I'd left behind had changed too. Driving along the streets I used to pass was nostalgic, especially for someone like me who enjoyed daydreaming while staring out the car window. It brought back old memories of how naïve I'd been about the future. But Bandung was too busy for my melancholy feelings. Traffic was everywhere, motorbikes overpowering the cars, people crossing the street without hesitation, and food hawkers enticing customers to park beside the road. Anyone could be easily forgotten here, yet I am always curious about what has changed in my hometown. I care too much.

A year had been too long. My parents squeezed me tight after I rang the doorbell. And there was my bedroom waiting as I entered the house. It looked more spacious than I remembered because my mother had tidied up my belongings, including the private folder where I'd put my photos and diaries. She did things this way to find out about my personal life discreetly. I did not grow up sharing feelings and thoughts with my parents. Writing a journal during my teenage years was my outlet to pour all my contemplation into freely. It was getting more difficult for my mum to discover what I had been up to since I'd moved overseas. My life snapshot had changed to digital form, and she was still stuck in my hard copy world.

My cousin is four years older than me, and he used to live at my parents' house, as his university was closer to my hometown. My bedroom was next to his room, which was now unoccupied since he had moved to Bali. I sneaked into his room to check on something I had discovered long ago in my teenage years. My secret sanctuary was still hidden in the cupboard; my cousin must have left it there when he moved out of my parent's house.

I was in senior high school when I became curious about his personal life. As he studied architecture in university, I often found interesting prototype buildings in his bedroom. His flamboyant outfits, such as polka dot shirts, oversized blazers, 80s neon jackets, and flare-legged pants, also fascinated me. One day after coming home from school, I checked his wardrobe and was intrigued by a locked shelf in a section of the cupboard. My detective mind emerged as I tried to find a way to open it. I removed the frame above it and squeezed my hand in to grab whatever items were hidden there. My adrenaline rushed when I saw what I had taken from the hidden cupboard. I sprinted to the living room. It was a collection of gay porn DVDs.

In junior high school, I'd realised that I was gay. But it wasn't until I watched gay porn that I learned about anal sex. Home alone time became something I looked forward to. It was my liberation time to re-watch the penetration scenes. They said it was unholy, but I indulged it anyway. Everything would be fine as long as I returned the DVD to the same position. My cousin did not notice that I'd also used his collection for my pleasure.

Because my mum enjoyed tidying up the room, it was only a matter of time before she spotted other hidden items. A couple of months after I found the gay DVDs, my mum discovered an old backpack in the corner of my cousin's bedroom. In it was a photo album containing a collage of topless male models he had compiled from magazines. I was not home when my parents stormed in, but I remembered what my sister said: "I heard everything from my bedroom. Dad was shouting and slammed the door. Mum was just crying because she was the one who confiscated those topless male images."

I do not have a close relationship with my cousin. He said

nothing to me and my sister when my parents discarded his collections. A couple of years after that incident, my cousin got married to a woman he met at university. He now has three kids from his marriage.

His life was the catalyst for my own life path. When I attended his wedding, I promised myself I would take a different approach to dealing with my sexuality. I knew it would be hard for my parents to accept my sexual orientation. They believed that homosexuality was a sin and should be fixed, and it was reflected in the way they had handled my cousin's situation. They would try to revert me to the cultural norms and religious beliefs if they knew I was gay. But it was my priority to find a way to be true to myself. If I did not, it would have been even harder for me to live a bogus life.

***

The initial excitement of visiting my hometown for my sister's wedding soon fizzled out. The first few days of my holiday were a constant test of my patience because family members repeatedly asked the same question: "When will you get married?"

"You are a good-looking young man and have a good career. What are you waiting for, Ozak?" My aunt caressed my face as if she felt pity.

There was little chance to share the story of how hard it had been for me to survive in a foreign land and finally get a job. My family members were too focused on the wedding euphoria, and marriage became a hot currency to check the value of someone's life. I wanted all the wedding preparations to be over as I had not flown across the ocean just to receive social judgement and be pressured into getting married.

A traditional ceremony was organised one day before the wedding reception. The first procession was intended as a blessing practice, held in the garden and witnessed by family and neighbours. My parents showered my sister with water and flowers while the community leader read the story of the parents' love for their children. The situation was unique because my younger sister was getting married before me. I also had to pour water as a sign that I, the older sibling who was still single, permitted her to get married.

The procession continued inside the house, where the religious leader prayed for a long-lasting marriage. My sister cried while kissing my parents' hands to ask for their forgiveness as part of the cultural tradition. It was time for them to let her go to live with the man she loved.

"This is for you." My sister gave me a parcel, a set of men's clothing, as the ceremony ended.

"Why?" I furrowed my brow.

"It is a gift in exchange for your marriage approval," my mother intervened.

"Oh, I see." I daydreamed. If I had known about this tradition, I would have asked for a return flight to Bali to make my support worth it.

At least 300 invitations had been sent for my sister's wedding. The reception would be a massive party as my big multicultural family was in charge. My dad comes from South Sulawesi province and has a Chinese Christian background, and my mum comes from West Java province and has a Muslim background. My family members alone took up a quarter of the seats at the wedding, and then there were my parents' colleagues and neighbours. It does not matter if the married couple does not know the guests. A wedding in Indonesia is all about family pride. The actual number of people who show up at the reception could even be higher than the number of invitations. It is common for guests to bring their spouses and kids. There is no such thing as a plus one. The more, the merrier.

"Jihan, please help me!" After an hour of phone conversation, I finally dared to ask a favour of my best friend. "You know how intimidating it is to attend a wedding alone. I feel like the world will be watching me the moment I step into the reception venue tomorrow," I sighed. "Would you please come to my sister's wedding and be my fake girlfriend for one day?" I lowered my voice to prevent my parents from overhearing.

I always thought fake relationships only happened in the movies, but now I was experiencing it. I introduced Jihan to family members on my sister's wedding day. She was the first person at university who knew I was gay. She accepted the invitation to be my fake girlfriend as it would be a good way for us to spend the whole day together. The last time we'd seen each other was at the airport for my farewell flight to Australia.

I hoped to have fun at my sister's wedding while enjoying the food and companionship. Instead, I had to play a game to avoid the "when will you get married" interrogation from family members. My defence mechanism was to bring false hope to everyone I met. None of them knew I was gay, and none of them understood that one of the reasons I wanted to live overseas was because of the social pressure to get married. My family members were surprised I had brought someone to the reception, as I'd never mentioned having a girlfriend.

"You are so pretty. I hope you will get married soon to

Ozak. Do not wait too long!" said my uncle.

"You must be smart if you have a pharmacy degree." My aunty was impressed with Jihan's educational background.

Jihan and I improvised our roles as a fake couple to answer any relationship queries from people at the wedding reception. We laughed in the corner of the hall about the love stories we made up spontaneously.

"I am having fun with you," I said to Jihan. "But I wonder how many gay men in Indonesia get married to women just because of social pressure." I looked at the ceiling. "One day of acting is already exhausting! I can't imagine those gay men who spend their whole life suppressing their sexual desire towards men and hiding it from their wives and kids." I sipped my drink as I knew I was being too passionate about sharing my thoughts with her.

"If someday I get married, it will definitely be to my future husband," I smiled. "I want to do it because I love someone wholeheartedly, not to please my parents and save the family's pride."

I made a good impression at my sister's wedding by showing up with a fake girlfriend. But I knew my parents would still consider me a burden, regardless of how financially independent I was, until I got married. The neighbours often asked them about my marital status, as they lived in a close neighbourhood. The burden came from their religion too. My parents accrued daily guilt that I was nowhere near marrying a woman.

"You know it is a parent's responsibility to see their children married. It is my sin if I do not remind you to get married," my mother said after my sister's wedding.

"Yes, I understand," I mumbled. Having an opinion when

parents were talking was perceived as being rebellious in my culture. I remained quiet as I listened to my mother's preaching.

"If you do not build your own family, who will care for you when you get older?" My mother held my hands.

The expectations would then continue, with having kids as the next item on the checklist. My parents wanted to have more grandchildren for their pride and to ensure that my children could take care of me when I was old like they expected me to take care of them.

I felt an itchy feeling listening to my mother because I wanted to tell her I was gay. But I thought about my cousin marrying a woman after my parents had condemned homosexuality. I held my thoughts back to avoid confrontation and left things unsaid for the better. But sooner or later, there would be words coming from my mouth. In the meantime, I was building my armour. I promised myself I would find the best way to come out to my parents, one fine day.

10 THE MARCHING BOYS

University is a pot of nostalgic memories. My four years of nostalgia were scattered around the Institute Technology of Bandung (ITB), Indonesia's first and oldest technology-oriented university. I returned there a couple of days after my sister's wedding to reunite with my lecturer. She had been willing to be a referee for my job application, and I owed her face-to-face gratitude for that.

"It is my pleasure to help my student. You are the only alumnus of Ocean Engineering who works in Australia so far, while others work in Norway." She put the boomerang gift on the table and gave me a thumbs-up.

The melodrama spun in my head as I continued to walk around the campus where I'd studied in 2005. Flashbacks are sometimes cruel. It only requires a simple trigger to time travel and find the emotion that is still there, lingering. Every corner of the colonial architecture building reminded me of romance stories. It was the period when I'd started to have encounters with fellow gay men.

I used to meet with a Javanese man at the campus entrance on the weekend. He lived in Jakarta and would drive 150 km all the way to Bandung to spend the night with me at the nearest hotel. He covered every bill to have my companionship, both physically and emotionally. The feeling was mutual. I adored him, a rugged and intelligent man in his late thirties.

The moment I first made love to him in a hotel room was unforgettable, witnessing a mature macho man reaching orgasm before my eyes. It was beautiful, and better than the scene on gay porn DVDs. His masculinity enraptured me, and I did not want to be cured of that. We liked to kiss and hug in the shower. I finally knew how it felt to be connected with a person on a deeper level than just having a conversation. I understood the benefit of having physical intimacy; I felt blissful. Whenever we were in the bathroom, I saw us as two men standing under the water flow with cosmic energy; holding each other's bodies felt like ecstasy.

There was no public affection when we went sightseeing around the city, although I badly wanted to hold his hand every time we walked side by side. Because of the age gap, we would introduce ourselves as uncle and nephew if we bumped into someone. I considered him my romance. But to him, I was just an affair. When the weekend ended, he would return to Jakarta where he lived with his wife. My memory taught me that not every man who married a woman was straight.

After visiting my university that day, I decided to meet with a local guy from a dating website. I wanted to plant a nostalgia seed in my hometown before returning to Australia. The wheel was turning, and this time I was the one who booked the hotel and sought a companion.

"We need to be very careful," I told my date as he arrived in the car park.

We made up a conversation about a football match when

we entered the lobby, to give the impression we were two heterosexual friends staying in twin beds. I bet the receptionist did not even notice us, but bringing a guy to a hotel room for sex made me guilty. I feared that if somebody reported us to the police, they would bust into the room as I'd seen on the news. After he left, I looked at the bathroom mirror and found my reflection living a double life again, hiding from the outside world. Concealing my identity, like in the old days of university, was the last thing I wanted to do after I'd gone all the way to Australia.

***

I had been in the closet since childhood. The conflict was classic; it was always between who I really was and what the social norm said I should be. The bullying at school, the stigma of the LGBTQIA+ community in Indonesia, and the sinner label from religious beliefs were things I considered a phase in life. Something I had to accept and move past. It left internal scars at the back of my mind.

The concept of gay pride did not exist in my dictionary until I moved to Australia. I learned it from the videos of the previous Sydney Mardi Gras. It was the first thing I wanted to do after I got back to Australia from my sister's wedding. The healing process had to start somewhere, and Sydney Mardi Gras was the right platform to do it. A celebration of freedom.

I did not want to go all the way to Sydney just for the party. My priority was to march and let my inner rebel out so I could be proud of myself and not be embarrassed about my sexual orientation. That was when I found a group online called Asian Marching Boys and Friends (AMBF). They had been marching since 1999 to promote the visibility of LGBTQIA+ Asians in

Australia. It took a private message on Facebook to pursue the possibility of joining the float.

"Hi there! I am an Indonesian gay man who lives in Perth. I have already booked a flight to Sydney to attend the Mardi Gras parade for the very first time. Is there any spot to participate in the march with your group? Thank you!"

The AMBF organiser accepted my request and gave me a briefing on their parade concept. It was about rainbow warriors to fit the 2013 Mardi Gras theme, Generation of Love. A total of sixty people were divided into six sub-groups representing the rainbow's colours. There was no pink, so I chose to be part of the red sub-group instead, symbolising bravery. We paid $50 to cover the costumes and learned the choreography to complement it. Everything we did was the gay version of a Christmas festive preparation, sassier and camper.

I would not miss Mardi Gras for the world. It was the opportunity to pop my cherry on discovering Sydney's gay life. I considered it my pilgrimage, and it all started by attending the Tower Party, where a massive queue awaited me. Luckily the organiser, who gave me a free ticket after we met online, was at the door.

"Hi Ozak, just come this way, darling!" He let me skip the line to access the rooftop lift.

It had a fabulous view of Sydney Tower Eye, not because of the Sydney city lights, but because seven drag queens were waiting near the bar.

"Can I take a photo with all of you, please?" I was surrounded by drag queens for the first time.

In Indonesia, drag queens have a derogatory image because they often hustle at traffic lights in exchange for money. The police sometimes target them at night due to alleged prostitution. The fate of drag queens depends on where they live; in one country they are seen as entertainers, and in other places, regarded as criminals.

After the party, I recovered from my hangover at the gay beach. Watson Bay is located in a remote area. It was a combination of a ferry trip and a half-hour walk through the forest to get there. When I bumped into shirtless guys, I knew I was going in the right direction. The landscape at the nudist beach impressed me. It had a tranquil atmosphere and pristine water. But I could not relax. I had been naked in the river at the hippy festival, but being surrounded by abundant fit gay men made me worried that I would get aroused. It turned out not to be an issue since many of them were making out behind the rocks. I observed from a distance, shy but curious at the same time. My testosterone was pumping hard when I exchanged eye contact. It was like watching an outdoor porn production. I felt so close to nature, not peaceful, but in a sensual way.

Sydney during Mardi Gras is very hot, not only because it is summertime, but also because of the action. One night, while staying at the backpacker hostel, I came across an Italian guy who was about to take the same lift. I squeezed in towards him and exchanged a friendly hello before we both got off at the male dormitory floor.

"How's your night been?" I stepped closer.

"A long day of sightseeing before the gay pride," he smiled.

"Alone?" I scanned the hallway.

"Yes, I'm staying in that dormitory." He shifted his body.

We kept flirting and talking in the corridor at midnight until we eventually kissed.

"Do you want to move?" He held my hand.

"Where?" I wondered. "Not in the bunk bed!"

"Follow me!" He pointed to the male bathroom.

***

Sydney Mardi Gras 2013 marked the 35th annual festival. The local government had made a rainbow crosswalk on Oxford Street as a temporary landmark and faced criticism when they decided to remove it after the parade. People took photos while it lasted. It was rare to be able to step on a rainbow that cost approximately $68,000.

The big day had finally arrived. I met with the AMBF crew at the designated meeting point four hours before the march. The drag queen led each sub-group with its representative colour. The colours drew the attention of the tourists who had arrived early on Oxford Street. The street had been barricaded, and the audience had to watch from the side of the road. They took photos and touched us as we walked, a celebrity moment for all of us.

"Everyone follow me!" The AMBF organiser raised his hand. "Don't forget to show your wristband to access the float area!"

We moved to the backstage location, where we lined up for the parade. We were one of the last groups to march. To kill time, we rehearsed countless repetitions of the choreography before the 1.5-km march began. The Mardi Gras crew constantly communicated with each float, ensuring they could move the groups on time. The clock pointed to 9 pm, and we could see the float in front of us finally moving forward. It was time to shine, sharing our fabulousness with the people on Oxford Street.

We emerged from the west side of Oxford Street. A massive crowd was cheering and waving as we entered the main road.

The atmosphere was full of hysteria, welcoming people like me. Never in my life had I felt so accepted.

"You are beautiful!" a girl shouted.

"Happy Mardi Gras, sexy!" a man smiled.

"Come here! Photo! Photo, please!" A group of teenagers raised their hands.

I closed my eyes and inhaled all the positive energy I felt until tears welled in my eyes. All these years, I had been waiting for this moment where I could own myself. I knew there would be a place where I could walk with pride.

At the beginning of the march, I started healing from the oppression of being gay I had experienced back in Indonesia. I walked proudly, remembering how far I had come.

I marched to remember the moment I chose to be a Pink Power Ranger while playing with the boys in my childhood.

I marched to remember that I'd bought a set of Barbie dolls at elementary school when other kids were playing soccer.

I marched to remember how I got my first girlfriend in junior school so my friends would not call me a faggot.

I marched to remember joining an Islamic youth organisation at high school, hoping I would be cured.

I marched to remember I'd spent endless nights at my university chatting with gay guys so we could meet up discreetly in an enclosed room.

I marched to remember that after graduating, I had to find my own path instead of marrying a woman like my peers.

I was not only remembering those moments when I marched. I also found myself contemplating the answer to the question that always came up when I faced a difficult situation due to my sexual orientation: "Why am I gay?" I would have a different world had I been straight. Perhaps I would just be settled in Indonesia and have even gotten married before my younger sister. Being gay had led me down adventurous roads that had brought me closer to myself. Being gay pushed me to look deeper into myself, face the beauty and ugliness of my reflection, and learn to love it all.

At the fabulous Sydney Mardi Gras, I was publicly out to reclaim myself as a proud gay man. I knew no one else could march on my behalf and carry the exact emotions I had on my shoulders. No one but me could walk for my own liberty.

11 THE CIRCLE OF FRIENDS

If a friendship could be transformed into an object, I would pick a birthday cake. It has to be there in the present. If it is only an emoji on a digital message, it is just an ache. It was the same with texts from friends and family back home. They could not ease the occasional loneliness of being in a foreign land. Every conversation on the group chat only reminded me that I was missing moments with them. Our daily routines had caused us to drift apart. They were there, and I was here, already in the process of losing our camaraderie.

It wasn't often that I revisited my friendship list. At least, not until I returned to Perth after attending Sydney Mardi Gras. It all started when I uploaded to Facebook a photo of me waving the rainbow flag while jumping shirtless, wearing red leggings. Whilst my family members received minimum updates on Facebook due to my adjusted privacy settings, coming out to my friends was still a significant milestone. It was a baby step on the journey of being true to myself.

"*That is gay propaganda!*" My university friend complained about the Mardi Gras photos through a private message. "*Ozak, it's not too late to ask forgiveness from Allah. Homosexuality is against Islam!*"

Unapologetic, I wrote a response to the Facebook post:

"Dear friends, to those of you who feel offended by this photo album, feel free to remove me from your friend list. I still respect who you are, but I don't need your acceptance. Things have changed, and we might have crossed onto a different path. Peace and love."

Having thousands of friends on social media did not guarantee a genuine friendship after all. Some were just acquaintances from school, and others from social networking events I'd met once. Those people were easy to let go of. But I had to be brutal and cull some close friends as they could not accept the version of me that did not match their beliefs. That was the cost of my coming out, and I refused to settle for less.

I cherished the past, those sweet recollections we'd had together. But some people were not meant to be for future memories. It is okay to leave the past bubble behind, and know they have walked away. One day, I knew I would understand my life path, and it did not matter what the person who opposed me thought. I should not have to depart from my own journey.

***

After I got a place to live and a job, a circle of friends was what I needed to complete my immigration settlement checklist. It was not about replacing long-lost friends. It was a continuity process. After all, things change in life. As an immigrant, friends are like extended family. They are the ones who provide emotional shelter through good and bad times, a sense of home without the roof.

My new friendship group was born through an outdoor camping group. Thirty-two people of different nationalities went for a trip to Kalbarri, north Western Australia, during the Easter long weekend. Within a week of the adventure, I had become close friends with six of them, including my straight crush. He stood out from the group with his athletic physique, a kite surfer who played the guitar. Along with his charm, he also did not have a problem with me being gay. My straight crush was the complete package.

We celebrated returning to civilisation by going to a gay club. One juicy moment was when I took my shirt off from too much dancing, and my straight crush followed my lead. A girl and I danced in between him, making a sandwich formation. He was not reluctant to be skin-to-skin with me, and I felt human. Back in Indonesia, many straight guys would think gay men were contagious. They would have felt disgusted if they were approached by gay men. They thought people like me were like predators, looking for any man to seduce.

"Do you want to hang out at my place and have a music jam session together?" my straight crush texted a few days later.

He lived one hour from the city centre and was willing to pick me up from my place. I sat on the front passenger seat next to him and tried to avoid making too much eye contact, hiding an obvious signal that I liked him. My excitement during the car ride was nothing compared to when I arrived at his place; no one else was in the house. My mood shifted to hopeless romantic mode when he showed me around his music studio. Saturday night, and it was just the two of us.

"It's easy to create a musical arrangement, you know. You just need to add things to the bar chart." He opened his music editing software.

"How do you normally get the inspiration to write the lyrics?" I sat next to him, shoulder to shoulder.

My straight crush was bombarded with questions. He could

talk about anything; I would still be his greatest listener. I was thirsty about anything on his mind. The temptation worsened as his cologne pulled me closer while we looked at the monitor together. We talked about music until late at night, but he occupied my mind with the way he spoke about his song and how he looked at me while waiting for my comment.

"You are more than welcome to sleep over on this couch." He stood up from the chair after shutting down the computer.

"Thanks!" I smiled at him, but deep down, it was a sour smile. I was expecting more than a couch.

"I'm off to bed now," he yawned, stroking his wavy hair.

"Where is your bedroom?" I was intrigued.

"Come with me." He opened the music studio door.

I was suddenly wide awake when I entered his cave. My evil side suggested I should tease him as we said good night. But I did not want to make any wrong moves. I left his bedroom and returned to the music studio instead, battling with my perverted thoughts. I kept wondering what he was doing in his bedroom, alone. It was the longest night I'd ever had, but I was proud of myself the next morning. I had not let my fantasy derail our friendship.

"*Hi, bro! Do you want to come for Sunday brunch at my place?*" he texted the following week.

There was a reward for being a good boy. My straight crush cooked in the kitchen in front of his mum, who was around that day. I felt special and flattered. I learned that my sexual orientation did not stop me from having a genuine friendship with a straight guy. I proved to myself that hanging out with my straight crush and having a bit of a bromance was just fine.

"How come he never cooks pancakes for me?" My straight

The Circle of Friends

crush's girlfriend slapped my shoulder when I told her about my brunch experience.

***

My circle of friends expanded when I received the invitation to join a dodgeball game from some friends. The opposition team of bogan men had hit me in the face with the ball on day one. My glasses did not break, but it wrecked my dignity. In the next match, I wore the leggings I'd used in Mardi Gras to make jumping and running around the court easier. It was an enlightening moment. There was no turning back.

"Way to go, mate!" My teammates commented on my outfit. Not only did I enjoy the functionality of it, but I also discovered the beauty of wearing leggings in different colours and patterns.

The blokey men dominated the sports venue and went there to do indoor futsal, softball, and weightlifting. There I was, the only gay man on the team. Sometimes I'd get frowned upon when I exited the male changing room wearing leopard-print leggings. But I focused on the positive side as most of them smiled when they looked at me. We were there to have fun. It was like in a Halloween match when I went shirtless in a leather harness, black leggings and devil makeup to get the best costume award. Even during sport, the staff could not resist the kinky look.

Dodgeball was not the only platform I used to make new friends. Singing has always been my passion, and I brought it to an open mic night. It was an excuse to gather my friends over a cheap pizza while they coped with my playlist and melody.

"We got a newcomer here. Give it up for Ozak!" The host called my name.

My first open mic at the gay bar in Perth was a bust. The moment I stepped on the stage, I felt like all eyes were on me. The echo of my own voice travelled from the speakers when I sang "Domino" by Jessie J as the opening act. Every note that came out of my mouth was a battle between emotion and heartbeat. The performance was not only for me. I sang for friends who were there to support and comfort me after I finished the song, having forgotten the lyrics and replaced them with *na na na na*.

Since my solo open mic debut, I started having jam sessions with my housemates in Bulwer Street, ten minutes from Perth city centre. Initially, the landlord liked to sit with us in the dining room to witness the house coming alive with music. But after a couple of weeks, she got disturbed by the excessive noise we made. "Can you please find somewhere else?"

I thought of creating a housemate acoustic band, where I sang, the Italian strummed the guitar, the French girl played the tambourine, and the Japanese guy became our cameraman. We signed up at the open mic night I used to go to. Our backpacker friends became groupies and jam-packed the venue. When the host granted us a $50 gift voucher at the end of the night as consideration of best performance, the bar transformed into an international brawl, fighting for free margherita and pepperoni pizzas.

"Do you want to busk on Sunday morning?" My Italian housemate kept me under his wing when he took my voice to Fremantle Market, beyond the open mic gig at the bar.

Busking in Australia means registration, and the local council gave us time to perform at the designated area. It was a revelation for me because in Indonesia busking is associated with poverty, a chance for homeless people to beg for money; it's not about talent and registration.

We started our Sunday performance at the coffee shop in exchange for free coffee and breakfast. Then we continued to busk in the market alleyway, where people passed by. Whenever I finished a song, my Italian housemate would give a short speech to the pedestrians.

"You are very wonderful. Your money too." He looked at the people while strumming his guitar. "Only if you want, okay? Only if you want." He opened the guitar case.

Singing in public and feeling close to the audience made my heart full. It was like being on the concert stage but without barricades. Our performance earned us $100 within an hour. We also got free juice in exchange for busking next to the stall owned by an Italian family. But busking was more than the money and free perks we got; it was an opportunity to make friends with fellow buskers and people in the market, outside of the corporate world I lived in during the week.

My life outside work became busy with camping, dodgeball and open mic nights. I stopped stressing about my work probation and visa expiration date. I always had something to look forward to after 5 pm and on the weekend. I enjoyed what Perth could offer and shared it with people I cared about. My confidence grew because I had a safe space regardless of my sexual orientation.

"Table for eight under Julia, please," my friend from the camping group said to the waiter.

We were having dinner at our favourite Korean barbecue after returning from a day trip to a winery. We ordered plenty of food like beef bulgogi, wagyu steak, marinated beef ribs, and kimchi. The smoke from the stove fuelled our appetite as we'd skipped lunch and drunk too much wine.

"Excuse me, can I have your attention?" Julia silenced the group in the middle of dinner. "Ozak, we got a message for you. Have a look at this video." She showed me her tablet.

My eyes focused on the screen. It appeared that my best friends in Indonesia had gathered in the park to wish me a happy birthday. It marked the first surprise birthday party I'd had since I'd moved to Australia.

"Happy birthday to you!" Another friend came to our table with the Black Forest cake. The people in the restaurant sang "Happy Birthday" as well.

My old friends in Indonesia and new friends in Australia became united on my birthday. I used a serviette to wipe away my tears, realising they'd made contact with each other to prepare the surprise party. The previous year, I'd spent my birthday alone in my bedroom, scrolling through photos on my phone to find happy memories.

I looked at the cherry on top of the cake. It reminded me that I was not anonymous in Australia anymore. I had people whom I could share the birthday cake with. Happiness comes from a support system with acceptance, and I felt blessed that I did not have to play hide and seek about my sexual orientation with them. They accepted my leggings obsession and saw me as an individual, not Ozak the gay one. Perth was no longer a city full of strangers. It had started to become my second home. The circle of friends made me feel like I belonged.

12 THE ENGINEER

"Go back to where you came from! You are stealing our jobs!"

Some people relocate across suburbs, cities or interstate to work for a better life. The minute they cross the international border, it becomes headline news. We all move to survive. But for immigrants, living in a foreign country is more than daily survival to get income and pay taxes. It is about satisfying the immigration rules in order to be legal.

Staying in Australia was my immigration saga. Some of my friends had been forced to leave the country because their visas had ended. My company was the source of hope that could support me once the initial 18 months of Subclass 476 – Skilled Recognised Graduate Visa expired. For this reason, work was my priority above the open mic, dodgeball, outdoor camping and other fun social activities. I went to the office every day as part of the immigration survival.

The stories about surviving and conquering the immigration challenges started right at the beginning of my career. There was one word that terrified me the most when I first joined the company: probation. It was another hurdle after getting the job in which I would have to prove that I deserved a permanent seat in the company.

I worked directly under the supervision of the engineering manager. My first assignment was dealing with a technical project using in-house finite element software to analyse the impact force of the fluid flow inside a rigid pipe. Subsea structural analysis was new to me. There was a moment when I was stuck and could not find the solution from the software simulation. But I was on work probation with no room for failure. I contacted the software team based in Ireland to beg for some ideas and incorporate their suggestions into my project. It took me a month and 26 revisions of the model to get reasonable simulation outcomes.

"You did it well. I appreciate you made a concerted effort to find the solution. Now I can see the pipe-in-pipe reaction force results make sense." My manager was satisfied with the analysis's conclusion.

Learning engineering software was one thing. The language barrier was a further obstacle I faced, as my English skills at that time were only up to the daily conversation level.

"I would encourage you to improve your English to meet technical engineering levels, both in speaking and writing," my manager said at my first performance review.

I did not talk much during discussions because of my unfamiliarity with the terminology in the subsea engineering field. Sometimes I did not know what to ask as I did not understand the context. The situation wasn't helped by my manager's Scottish accent, which I struggled to understand. Besides, my ears were flooded by my colleagues' Australian and Irish accents all at once.

Every day was about self-improvement. I turned on the radio to listen to the news and read previous engineering technical reports to sharpen my English. My bedroom walls had transformed into a gallery of paper notes of the new words I discovered daily. The benchmark of my progress was measured when I finally had an English conversation with friends in my dreamland.

The work probation did not only haunt me from Monday to Friday during office hours. I took the initiative and spent extra hours on the weekend learning subsea engineering theory and the software. But I made one mistake at the start. The alarm started ringing when I entered the building using my employee card. A pre-recorded voice instructed me to enter the code at the door. And I did not know about it. The spontaneous reaction I took when I heard the alarm was running out of the building in panic.

"Can I see your ID, please?" The security officer arrived at the office within a few minutes and observed me from head to toe, judging the combination of my shorts, t-shirt and sandals.

"Hold on a second." I put my slushy drink on the ground and grabbed my wallet from my back pocket.

"So, you work here then?" He checked my identity card.

"Yes, I do," I nodded.

"Why didn't you enter the security code to turn off the alarm?" He returned my card.

"I am a new employee and do not know the combination numbers." I gave him puppy dog eyes to indicate that I was innocent.

"No worries, but I still have to report this to the building management. It's a procedure." He saluted me.

My manager heard about the incident on Monday from the receptionist.

"You went to work on the weekend, didn't you?"

The first feeling I had was pride; my manager had noticed I was trying to work hard. As a new employee still on probation, I was aiming to make a positive impression.

"Next time, enter this number." He handed me the code to access the office outside business hours.

Working at the smallest sister company meant everyone could easily monitor my daily performance. At that time, there were twelve workers coming from Ireland, Scotland, Germany, France, and Australia. I was the only one from a developing country and still carried the Indonesian work ethic mindset. I arrived at 7.30 am and left the office only after my boss did. I would keep reading random technical reports, even though I had finished my tasks that day. I was a yes man, especially in meetings, to avoid any confrontation. I kept my personal life private while my colleagues shared their weekend activities. Until my mentor Daniel, half Australian and half Taiwanese, told me to relax.

"Probation is not only about proving your technical capabilities. The company wants to see whether you fit into our team environment," Daniel said, acknowledging the cultural differences between Western and Eastern work cultures.

I switched within days. I left whenever I finished work, joined the morning walk to the coffee shop, and went to sundowner drinks on Friday afternoons to mingle. My technical engineering skills were kept on top of, my written and oral communication skills improved, and interaction with the team members was maintained. I could not think of any other development that I'd missed to pass my probation.

"Please remind us a couple of months before your current

visa expires so we can process your working visa application." My engineering manager handed me the performance letter at the beginning of the year.

That piece of paper allowed me room to breathe. It was a green light that I had passed the probation period, and metamorphosed me into a permanent employee. Another milestone was achieved on my immigration journey through a combination of perseverance and patience. However, there was still a long way to go. My 18-month visa was still ticking, and the renewal decision was still pending.

***

My career highlights at work were when I got assigned to one of the most significant projects in the oil and gas industry under the supervision of a senior engineer from Germany. It involved the design of flexible risers attached to the FLNG (Floating Liquefied Natural Gas) vessel located in the Indonesian Sea. My job became a contribution to my motherland. Through this opportunity, I shared the workload between the Jakarta and Perth offices, in the same way I split my identity between these two countries.

The FLNG project boosted my career progress as it ran for a year. The typical project in the consultancy usually lasted for three months, with each consultant charging an hourly rate to the client. How many hours we could book in for the project measured our productivity. I did not have to worry about filling in my weekly timesheet. Having a long-term assignment made my productivity score higher, as I had billable work of forty hours each week.

The project pressure increased day by day, and it was getting more complicated because stakeholders in Indonesia and Australia fought for their own interests. My German supervisor gave me the structural analysis task and let me find the solution independently. He was always busy, either on the phone, in a meeting, or writing emails every time I went to his cubicle to ask questions. There was one time when we finally discussed the results, and I will never forget what he did.

"The compression force along the touchdown area is presented in this plot." I showed him my findings.

"Why didn't you discuss the methodology with me?" He crushed up my paper and threw it into the rubbish bin.

"I tried to explain it to you. But you did not have time whenever I came to your desk." My blood pressure went up.

"Fuck off!" He left me at my desk.

The whole office went quiet. My other colleagues around me buried themselves at their desks. I was stunned. I just sat on the chair, feeling the room temperature suddenly increase to above 30 degrees. My face was boiling, and the only thing I could hide was my tears because I managed to inhale and exhale at a constant pace. But I kept wondering what people had thought when they'd heard my supervisor swear at me. They'd witnessed my dignity shatter in a blink of an eye, destroyed by hurtful words.

Daniel came to me. "Are you okay? Let's grab a coffee."

"I think I need some time alone."

I left my desk to get some fresh air. In the park, I called my fake girlfriend, Jihan.

"I had enough! I was humiliated in front of everyone when he shouted and swore at me," I cried. "I want to quit and return to Indonesia. I am such a failure." I continued sobbing.

"Don't give up! I know it's hard. But you are lucky. People

back home want to be in your position and work overseas, and you have the opportunity to build your dream." Jihan comforted me across the ocean with her soft voice.

It was not about how strong I was. I had been pushing myself hard since I'd joined the company, adjusting to the work culture, language, and new knowledge. But while I'd learned new things, I'd also accumulated a tonne of mental stress. All the little struggles at work had become a ticking bomb. It only took one solid punch, in this case, the swear word from my supervisor, for me to explode. Quitting was an abrupt escape mechanism in response to that incident.

After pouring my feelings out to Jihan over the phone, my mind felt clearer, and I went back to my desk carrying puffy eyes hidden behind my glasses. I did not leave the company; instead, I carried on working until 5 pm. It was the slowest countdown to the end of the day I'd ever experienced.

I shared the issue with my engineering manager the following day. To my surprise, he'd also noticed my German supervisor's aggressive attitude at the office as he swore a lot at his cubicle during the workday.

"You did the right thing to inform me. Let me handle this. What he did is unacceptable in our office culture," the manager reassured me in a meeting room after I told him the chronology of the event.

My German senior engineer asked me to go to the meeting room with him a few days later.

"I genuinely apologise for what I did." He lowered his voice. "I admit I was so stressed out because of the project load. It has been tough few weeks lately, dealing with this client."

I appreciated his decision to have a face-to-face conversation with me. I was touched because he apologised for his temper, even though he held a higher position than me in the company. And that was more than enough for me to move on. I learned that in Western culture, everyone is treated equally and respectfully. If my boss in Indonesia had shouted at me, I would most likely have kept it to myself, respecting the company's hierarchy.

***

Being a subsea engineer to me is about prestige. It helped boost my confidence as an immigrant every time I went to a social event, especially the part when people asked, "What do you do?" Most people I met did not understand the word "subsea" — or perhaps just how I pronounced it. The conversation dynamic would change until I mentioned oil and gas. "It is a well-paid job!" they often said.

Being a subsea engineer is also about balance. It allowed me to explore my right brain to keep up with my left brain, which had been squeezed after sitting in front of the computer the whole day. I accumulated healthy stress from the workloads and channelled it through my creative platforms. I took Latin dance classes, performed at open mic nights, and wore pink jeans to the office as my fashion statement on casual Fridays.

But most of all, being a subsea engineer is about hope. It was the key to staying in Australia when my initial 18-month visa ended. Just three months before my visa was due to expire, the Human Resources staff finally contacted me.

"It is a selective process. Our company had to prove to the government that we could not find an Australian worker for your nominated position as a subsea engineer." She corrected her glasses as she spoke. "We also have to pay your training budget to the government every year. But don't worry. Our company will sponsor you under a Subclass 457 – Temporary Work Skilled Visa. It will be quick, as you are a high-skilled migrant." The Human Resources officer handed me the visa documents for me to sign.

"Thank you so much!" I took a bow while I sat on the chair.

"You can apply for a permanent residence visa too once you hold the 457 Visa." She smiled.

"How long do I need to wait?" I tilted my head.

"Two years, I think." She looked at her computer.

Having a company to sponsor my working visa was the answer I had not had when I'd decided to book a one-way ticket to Australia. And I thanked myself for following my inner voice at that time, despite the unknown. When I really listened to it and felt it, I knew it would guide me to my destiny.

Many things could happen in the two years until I became eligible to apply for a permanent residence visa. I realised I would have to endure daily challenges at work, but at least I could see my immigration light at the end of the tunnel. It was bright, and its glow reminded me to keep walking towards it. One day, I would reach my ultimate goal of living in Australia indefinitely. I would find my permanent address eventually, the home I had been waiting for.

13 THE ASIAN

First is the accommodation, the second is the job, and the third is the circle of friends. But when someone moves overseas alone, there is a fourth item on the list that could make the immigration narrative complete: a better half.

Around the world, people were suffering from war, hunger and natural disaster. Meanwhile, my first-world problem was finding love. I'd flown across the ocean to be comfortable in my own skin and had made peace with my sexual orientation. But accepting a same-sex attraction did not guarantee love would arrive at my front door. I'd sung at the open mic night, played dodgeball, and joined a camping group. I worked as a subsea engineer and secured my visa to be an independent immigrant. Every day I tried to become a better version of myself as people said, "Love yourself first." But still, I could not see the love light coming towards me that I thought I deserved.

Here was how it went: I woke up, spent eight hours at work, and did not want to find myself alone in my bedroom after 5 pm. I would then pick a range of activities to do in order to return home late. But nightfall would eventually approach. At the end of my day, I would lie on the bed with my phone until I went to sleep. It was fine for days, weeks and months. But after more than a year, I started to think, *"When will someone wake up next to me at 6 am to share my morning routine, fighting for cereal brands and fixing my shirt collar? When will I come home from work to find someone on the couch I can cuddle to while debriefing after a long day? When will I have pillow talk with someone before sharing a goodnight kiss?"*

There were friends with whom I could exchange conversation and hugs. But their intimacy had boundaries that did not suit my libido in winter. There were things I wanted to feel skin to skin, under the blanket, until I was out of breath. There were melancholic sides of me, full of midnight thoughts, random facts and sporadic ideas that I wanted to share without losing eye contact and warm hands. This was me, an immigrant who was longing for a boyfriend.

Online dating had always been my best practice when it came to seeking romance. The first time I'd logged in to a gay dating website was way back when I was at university in Bandung, Indonesia. It was a safe platform to connect with people like me who had already endured a hard life in the heteronormative society. We all hid in the real world but emerged on the chat forum, where I spent hours screening the profiles and arranging meetups in the deserted evening.

The more time I spent online, the more I encountered profiles stating, *"No effeminate guys!"* I often received messages asking bluntly, *"Are you masculine?"* as if it was part of a verification system, and giving the correct answer would make a huge difference to how far the conversation progressed. *"Yes, definitely!"* indicating that I was masculine, although I was not sure what the concrete parameters were on this.

I reflected on my upbringing at school; a feminine boy was an easy target for bullies. The effeminate sentiment passed into the gay dating scene in Indonesia, where most users wanted to be portrayed as straight as possible to avoid being identified as an outcast by society. I invented the concept of straight acting, where I would talk in a bass voice, avoid dressing up in bright colours, and make my gestures stiff when I met gay guys. I sacrificed being myself to get attention from the people I liked.

Finding love on the online dating scene in Indonesia brought me endless nights full of lust. I went from one man to another, hoping I could find the connection I desired. I wished my touch, kiss, and warm body could transform lust into love every time I hooked up with someone. But the lust was temporary and never turned into romance; it only accompanied me as I passed the sleepless nights.

***

When I migrated to Australia, I used a gay dating app, Grindr, to connect with local gay guys. I expected the online world would be a friendly space. But there was a harsh reality every time I scrolled through member profiles. I repeatedly found *"No Asians"* comments on their accounts. I started to question whether there was something wrong with me. I correlated the *"No Asians"* with the *"No effeminates"* sentiment I'd experienced in Indonesia. I'd entered a community where preferences created a hierarchical pyramid, and I was pushed to the bottom of it. I could act straight to get through from the *"No effeminates"* filter, but it was a dead-end when dealing with the *"No Asians"*. I could not change my race and pretend to be a Caucasian man. I could not hide my face, skin and body form. I'd lost my battle in the online dating game as I believed I was an unwanted object.

I had never been so aware of my body features until my experience dealing with the *"No Asians"*. I analysed my physique, genital size, and skin colour to judge my attractiveness. I was anxious about my image, not satisfied with my scrawny 175cm, 60 kg reflection. The gym became a refuge to redeem myself, hoping I could improve the probability of finding love. I cared too much about the online version of me, wanting to fit the box and meet the standards of male beauty I perceived: muscle and macho. Every day I would assess my progress by looking at my reflection in the bathroom mirror as a post-workout ritual. I learned how to find the best angle to show off my six-pack in selfies taken while holding my breath. My ego wanted me to be at the top of the pyramid. I taught myself that being effeminate was wrong and that being a masculine, muscular gay man was the way to survive.

"Are you on steroids?" I contacted a personal trainer on Grindr.

I was amazed when he visited me at my place. He had a bodybuilder persona that I wanted to have. His muscles, twice the size of mine, convinced me to take steroids, as I could see the results in him.

"I already sent you a file about the steroids, including their effects." He closed his laptop as we sat next to each other.

"Got it!" I adjusted my glasses while checking my inbox.

"I didn't want to pressure you and give you my personal recommendation. Just make your own decision from the information I've given you. I'm here to provide insights, not sell a product." His bulky biceps flexed every time he moved his hands while talking.

"May I know your personal reason for taking steroids?" I

looked at his sweaty shoulder muscles as he was covered by a tight singlet.

"Well, it is part of my job to attract clients. As a personal trainer, my persona matters, and I want to be muscular to gain their trust." He pointed to his body.

"Are you not afraid of the risk?" I slowed down my question.

"I've been using steroids for fifteen years. I take them for a few months, then recover for a while. I don't care if I have a low sperm count because I don't want to have kids," he smiled.

"I see." I nodded.

"But you need to be ready to have a strict diet program, get enough sleep, do frequent exercise, and spend hundreds of dollars per week to buy the steroids. Behind the results, there are endless commitments to make. It is not a magical transformation after all!" He looked at me.

I contemplated whether I wanted to inject steroids over a long-term period and take pills, as if I were ill, to get my desired body image. The hardcore fitness regime scared me as I wanted to keep the possibility of having guilty pleasures open, such as partying at midnight, drinking alcohol, and eating greasy foods. There was no tight deadline to become muscular. It made sense to take a long journey and include exercise as part of my lifestyle after spending all day in front of computers at work. My pondering had shifted the motivation to exercise from battling body insecurity to getting active, and kept aesthetic results as a long-term bonus.

The decision not to take steroids was a small step in making peace with my physique. I began to seek out muscular Asian figures for fitness inspiration, but they were difficult to find in the advertising of a Western country. My enthusiasm was restored when I finally discovered some Asian role models I could look up to on social media. There were several accounts compiling Asian men's pictures from around the world, and I could see the definition of sexiness that resonated with me. Representation matters in the end.

I could not force someone's desire regarding who they wanted to sleep with. I did not want to be with a person who did not want me back. But the *"No Asians"* to me was not about a preference; it was a broad generalisation. It was an inconsiderate move that was often overlooked. In the end, words can empower or destroy people.

After a while, I learned not to be bothered when I encountered a profile saying, *"No Asians"*. I got used to it, the way gay guys get used to being called faggot by their peers at school. It was that feeling, painful, but I could brush it off. I saw it as one of the risks of being on Grindr, like gambling with bad bets. Finding a compatible match was still one in a million.

One time, I received a message from a guy who had written *"No Asians"* on his profile.

"I thought you did not like Asian men," I replied to his message.

"You are the exception because you are muscular and have darker skin," he responded.

"It is still an absurd reality knowing that, as well as dealing with homophobia from society, I also have to face toxic masculinity and racism within the gay community from people like you! How can you be sure that Asian users are into you when you say no to them first?" I read his profile description one more time before I blocked his account. Furious.

***

Dance heals the soul. It was something I'd learnt way back in the hippy festival under the full moon. I would take myself dancing to the gay club after midnight as my self-love ritual. There was a dance monologue among the people on the podium. Under the shimmering disco ball, I delivered a self-affirmation that I am worthy. The music helped me to connect with my body every time I followed the rhythm. I let it sweat without my clothes and kept my eyes closed while feeling sexy and raw.

I repeated my dance monologue every Saturday night. The dance floor was a therapeutic place. One early morning, I walked back home feeling exhausted from dancing. I dragged my feet and tried to keep my balance as I walked under the influence of alcohol. I arrived at the front gate of my house after an hour-long drunken walk, and a simple revelation came to me: I could not be too cruel to myself. My body accompanied me dancing. My body brought me safely back home from the club every weekend. My body covered my soul as I fell asleep. My body is a creature, not an online object.

The following day, I asked my friend to take shirtless photos of me and to write several statements on my body using red lipstick. Each sentence represented my experience with Grindr.

"*My body is not welcome*" was written on my chest.

"*No Asians*" was written on my forehead.

"*People often confuse having types with the freedom to shoot others down. You said, 'It is just what I prefer'*," was written on my back.

"*I refuse to become what you call normal*" was written on my arms.

The wounds from gay apps became art pieces. I posted the photos on my blog and social media to make my friends aware of what I had been through. My body turned into my voice in the name of visibility and vulnerability.

The last thing I wanted to do was feel sorry about being a gay Asian man. If some people believed I belonged at the bottom of the preference pyramid on a dating app, if our beauty was not for everyone, then all I cared about was to be beautiful in my own way while lifting myself up. I would demolish the pyramid into a flat surface where each person could appear as the headline act.

I know that many people in the online world deserve more than a filter. There is a human with real feelings and tender emotions behind every digital profile.

14 THE GAY TRIP

Being single could be daunting, with the occasional feeling of being incomplete, despite having a promising career and lovely friends. During my time as a single gay man, my life direction forced me to grow internally and learn how to be content with myself. It left me with no choice but to embrace my singlehood, which I did. I rode it hard by booking a European winter holiday for the first time. I thought, let me be wild and unleash my fantasies while I am single. Let me unwrap the gay scene in other continents. Europe could be a sweet remedy for the *"No Asians"* statement I'd encountered in the Land Down Under.

I did not ask Europe to be gentle when I arrived. I wanted a rock and roll gay trip from the starting point. The notifications from Grindr inundated my phone from the moment I first logged in at Frankfurt International Airport. Forget about the jetlag and six hours' time difference; I was exuberant, screening the messages in my inbox as if I were sitting next to the sushi train.

"Come over?" I texted one of the guys who happened to be in the same hotel.

It was three degrees in Frankfurt when I landed, but my room temperature increased from the welcoming actions of this six-foot-tall bearded Italian guy. It was a pleasant warm-up at the start of my trip, and made me want to explore more. I'd gathered quick information on the phone about the nearest gay bar to my hotel, not knowing what to expect when I got there. Some people looked at me when I entered—fresh meat for them. It was a small venue with a hundred-person capacity, and it would have been obvious if I had left the premises immediately due to my nerves. I tried to play it cool to have just one bottle of beer.

Friday night was busy. A couple of groups gathered near high round tables; people had to squeeze between them to get to the hallway. While I sat on the last seat next to the topless bartender, I noticed the corner area where people were coming and going from a particular room. It was definitely not the toilet, as I had thought at the beginning. I drank half of my beer before checking it out. There was no door, but the room was dark, even from the outside. Some of the men stood against the wall, pulling their zips up. I was intrigued and went inside.

There was no conversation whatsoever, but I could hear some people moaning. A person in front of me suddenly grabbed my crotch. I could not see any faces in the complete darkness, but I let the invisible guy grind his arse on my jeans. Another man groaned louder than before to confirm that I was in a dark room for a quickie. I'd already had some action in my hotel room; therefore, I left with my silly grin, realising what I had just discovered. On the first night of my holiday, I learned that it was normal to have a cruising sex area, even in a small gay bar in Germany.

I left Frankfurt for Paris the following day. A gay bed and breakfast apartment in the gay district, Le Marais, waited for me. My excitement disappeared when I finally entered the room on the third floor. It was smaller than the pictures I had seen on the website; a living space with a shared kitchen, a bathroom and a bedroom. Five posters of topless gay men under the reflection of the dim lights decorated the wall next to the television, which somehow radiated a brothel atmosphere.

"These are the two bunk beds," said the host when we entered the bedroom.

"Ouch!" My feet stumbled, hitting the steel bed behind me.

"We will have the place to ourselves. The other guest checked out today." He pointed out to the top bunk where I would sleep.

I rolled my eyes, realising I was the only guest that night. Once I dropped my luggage, I kept minimal interaction with him and went out to a gay bar. I decided to book a last-minute hotel nearby after I got a creepy vibe from him. After all, he wore a t-shirt that read *"Cum in me, bro!"*

"I am going to stay at my friend's place," I lied to the host when I left the next morning, even though I'd already paid for a four-night stay.

Although I did not get the whole experience of staying in gay accommodation in Paris, I still made friends with local people. Thanks to Grindr, I got invited to meet a handsome and well-built Parisian guy. His address was my tourist attraction. I discovered a neighbourhood with Haussmann architectural buildings along the Seine River, which I would not have noticed if I had not visited him.

"*Bonjour!*" The Parisian guy opened the apartment door.

His stubbly beard and strong jaw caught my eye. As well as his looks, he comforted me from the six-degree winter weather by serving hot green tea.

"How's it going?" I tried to open up the conversation.

"*Je vais bien, merci!*" he replied.

It took me half a glass to realise that the Parisian guy could not speak English. He'd used a mobile app to translate all the conversations when we had chatted initially. I sipped my tea when I ran out of words. We smiled at each other, both lost in translation. At some point, he walked to his bedroom, and I followed him from behind as I did not have to translate the clue to get laid. We used body language not only to communicate but also to have physical contact. We flexed our muscles to find out who was the strongest. Ignore the language barrier. There were no words required when two men finally wrestled on the bed.

My European trip continued to the Netherlands to meet Aunty Heidy. She is technically my cousin, but we have such a huge age gap. My father is the youngest of ten siblings, and my rich oldest uncle had taken his family to settle down in the Netherlands as political refugees. My father said that Aunty Heidy had visited Indonesia when I was a child, but she was a long-lost family member to me.

Aunty Heidy lived in a small village near the Belgian border. I was just in time for her daughter's birthday party. I stayed overnight at her place while getting to know my extended family and enjoying Indonesian food. The following day, Aunty Heidy and I had lunch together.

"You know your mum doesn't like me." She spoke while

we ate leftover *rendang,* a rich and tender coconut beef stew.

"Oh, why is that?" I put my spoon and fork on the plate.

"Your dad wanted a *Playboy* magazine. So I sent it by post from here to Indonesia. However, your mum somehow found the magazine underneath the bed. She was agitated and wrote a letter to me saying that what I did was inappropriate as a family member." She covered her mouth with her right hand, laughing. "The Netherlands is more open than Indonesia. For example, my sister divorced her husband in Jakarta and escaped here because she is a lesbian." Aunty Heidy changed her tone of voice.

"Oh, really?" I struggled to say a word. My mouth was full of rice.

"I accept her as long as she is happy." She looked at me.

I sipped water and stopped for seconds, pondering my response. "Actually, I'm gay too. One of the reasons I'm spending the holiday in Europe is to explore the gay scene here." I leant towards Aunty Heidy.

"I think if you tell your father, he will be okay. Judging by the *Playboy* magazine incident, your mum seems like a conservative Muslim woman." Aunty Heidy moved her hands around her face, referring to the hijab, my mum's veil.

My gay trip became special because I'd finally come out to a family member for the first time, and it had happened spontaneously over food and without tears. I felt relieved to share a part of me with her. I just wished my parents could someday accept me like my Aunty Heidy did.

***

Cologne in Germany was the next stop of my holiday, where I stayed with a high school friend.

"I know that you are gay!" Regina stuck her tongue out.

"Bitch, please!" I snapped my fingers twice in her face.

"Your ex-girlfriend was my best friend! Here you are a few years later." She grabbed my shoulders and shook my body.

We spent time together during the day visiting Cologne Cathedral, and she set me free during the evening to explore the fetish club that was hosting a leather party. My leather fantasy started when I discovered Tom of Finland's book in a sex shop back in Sydney. He is known for art sketches capturing gay muscular men wearing leather and military uniforms. Inspired by his artwork, leather fetish became an alternative scene in the gay community where men expressed themselves by wearing leather outfits and channelling their kinky side.

My exploration of the leather fetish club commenced in the underground area where private cubicles were set up to cater to people's actions. Passing through the sex room felt like walking into a maze. Sometimes it led me to a no-through road, a porn video lounge, or just to horny men standing next to the door waiting for prey. Nobody was talking; it was all about eye contact. I spent the first half an hour wandering around to see how many people noticed me. I wanted to check my thirsty ego, the feeling of being wanted.

Sex was transactional here. People could do anything behind the cubicle wall if consent had been established. The more I roamed, the more desire accumulated. And then there he was, a sexy German man wearing head-to-toe leather, standing in the corner of the hallway under red lamps. I counted my steps and marked him as the target, maintaining eye contact. He did not move, so I checked his personal space by squeezing my chest against his. He exhaled until I felt the warm air around my face.

I pressed him up against the wall and gave him a solid tongue kiss before I grabbed his hand and tugged him into the nearest cubicle.

"Do you want to come to my place?" He put on his leather jacket when we exited the playground area two hours later.

It was 2 am when I checked my phone. Time did really fly when I was with him in the cruising zone. It was a late night, and I needed to make a logical decision about his invitation.

"Let's do it!" My fantasy won, and I agreed to go with him, even though I had no clue where he lived.

I got into his car and hoped that everything would go well.

We were still on an empty highway after half an hour of driving. Then, my instinct awoke: *"What if he kidnaps me?"*

I did not let my sleepiness control my body to be alert if anything wrong happened. After an hour-long journey, we finally arrived at his apartment. It turned out he lived in a small town, Neuss, near Dusseldorf. It was not even in Cologne. No wonder the trip to his place had taken forever.

"Who is your master?" I pulled his leather jacket towards my chest when we entered his bedroom.

We carried on with our leather kinks on the bed. That night, my intuition led me to find the leather man, my own Tom of Finland, which I did not regret.

***

Germany had taught me about the darkroom at the gay bar and the leather fetish club. It had stretched my sexual boundaries in many ways. But I still had Berlin as the ultimate stop, the hometown of the infamous techno club, Berghain, and the gay sex club next to it, The Laboratory.

The Laboratory has a specific theme every night based on a

fetish dress code like leather, rubber, and sportswear. There is also a particular theme based on sexual activities, like the pissing night for people into golden showers and the fisting night for people who like deep anal penetration.

"It is a naked night," said the security guard.

I showed him my passport. "Can I get a plastic bag for my clothes, please?"

I did not have a problem with nudity, thanks to my experience at the hippy festivals and nude beaches in Australia. What shocked me when I went inside was the orgy happening in the open spaces of the club without discretion. I watched hundreds of naked men full of testosterone having sex in every corner. There was one guy surrounded by men in 360-degree directions. When I got closer, most of them were not using condoms. It was a wild bareback sex party.

I sat on a concrete block, drinking beer and processing the scene of lustful men around me. My conservative mind popped up. I did not have sex there because I was too paranoid about getting a sexually transmitted disease. All I could think of was the Australian permanent residence visa requirements. My application most likely would be rejected if the medical check showed I was HIV positive. I could not get aroused at the bareback orgy party, but at the same time, I was fascinated watching men having sex in the industrial building under the dim lights. It looked like I was in hell, surrounded by sin and pleasure. I felt guilty yet good.

The club next door, Berghain, hosted a three-day non-stop party to celebrate the new year. I dared myself to get inside the following day. I'd heard it was arduous to pass the screening from the infamous bouncer, Sven Marquart, who often rejects patrons without an explanation. There is even a whole online thread discussing getting into the club.

The queue was hundreds of metres long when I arrived. I wore dark yellow leggings, leather boots and a jacket on the night of judgement. The frostiness bit my skin and cut through my leggings. But somehow, it eased my facial expression and allowed me to remain impassive and radiate a "like I care" attitude. Minute by minute, the queue meandered towards the club entrance, and I could see lots of people getting refused by the bouncer, who was only using his body gestures. He did not say a word until I finally faced him.

"How many?" he asked me in German.

"One," I responded with my hand.

He opened the door and let me in without saying anything further.

"Don't take any photos or videos inside the club, okay?" Another staff member pointed his finger between my eyes.

I was filled with the emotion of coming home to a place I had never been before, but the venue atmosphere felt familiar to me. In my past life, I must have lived in ancient Rome and lived a hedonistic life. There were glimpses of people making out and having sex just near the cloakroom. The sound of techno music guided me to the main stage on the second floor, where people were dancing in their own world. I stood in the middle of the crowd having a dance orgasm. The rhythm, the volume and the lighting transported me into a different dimension.

Berghain was a utopian land. There was a discovery in every corner of the industrial building. I entered the third floor and encountered another zone for dark techno, a cubicle area for private sex, and a darkroom for men cruising. Before this, I could not have imagined being in a nightclub where people could do whatever they wanted without encountering brawls or other anti-social behaviour. The beat of techno tracks had united all.

I indulged myself with the music on the main stage area, finding my own zone with eyes closed. My mind flew high, following the rhythm orchestrated by the maestro DJ. I threw both hands in the air. It was a self-celebration, and it was a spiritual journey. It was a liturgy on the dance floor until the sun came up.

Exploring the European gay scene for a month was a key part of opening my boundaries. It was such a radical way to express my sexuality and dark fantasies. I came to realise that I deserved more than the *"No Asians"* statement. My persona was too sharp to be touched by those who could not appreciate pleasure in the form of pain. I knew where I felt welcomed as a gay Asian man and as a person who treasured the fetish scene. But my permanent residence dream waited for me in Australia. I returned to the Land Down Under as a different version of myself, knowing I had graduated with a kinky European degree.

15 THE BLAZING SWAN

Just be who you are, people said. But I do not wake up in the morning suddenly knowing how to be who I really am. There were moments when I tested myself in uncomfortable situations. Reflecting on my latest European trip alone, I had been terrified of making eye contact with the bouncer at Berghain in Berlin. I had been nervous about wearing my leather uniform on the train to go to the fetish club in Cologne. I had been conflicted about coming out to Aunty Heidy in the Netherlands. However, I'd stood up. I allowed myself to be authentically vulnerable, even in intimidating circumstances. Because that is part of finding out who you are, fully expressing yourself, no matter what it looks like. To be who you are is to be radical in self-expression and keep the burning energy inside alive.

"Have you heard about Burning Man?" Goldy, my non-binary friend, took out their phone.

"Is it a band?" I looked at the phone screen.

"Burning Man is an event in Nevada where people create a temporary world for about a week and leave no trace after it finishes. There are no guest stars, shops or any commercial transactions." They showed me some of the pictures.

"That is in the USA, too far!"

"There will be the first regional Burning Man event soon in Western Australia! It is called Blazing Swan!" They squeezed my shoulder.

"Cool, cool, cool." I nodded a few times.

"Let me introduce you to Clara, the founder of Camp Unicorn, this weekend, okay?" They made eye contact with me, and their rainbow glitter eyeshadow caught my attention.

Blazing Swan is an alternative community where radical self-expression is part of its ethos and principles. Like Burning Man, it ends with the ritual of a burning effigy, an iconic reminder to keep the creativity going even after the event ends. There are theme camps in Blazing Swan, which are basically an experiment of a temporary establishment. One of them is Camp Unicorn, a queer-friendly group that likes to dress up looking fabulously magical with bright colours, glitters, sparkles and horns. It is like a cult where they worship and believe that unicorns are real.

"There are many ways to contribute, babe." Clara opened her notebook, explaining some of the preparations needed for the Blazing Swan.

"We need to set up the communal kitchen and the dome for a chill-out area, find craft materials, and transportation to the field location. There will be a few meetings to discuss our main gifting in the upcoming weeks. You should come, babe." She tapped my thigh.

"Gifting?" I scratched my head.

"It is the term for contributing to the Blazing Swan community. In our case, we'll set up a unicorn costume library where people can borrow outfits during the event, and we'll also organise the Unicorn March to celebrate the inner unicorn that lies in everyone's soul. Who doesn't like unicorns, babe?" Clara stroked her purple hair whenever she mentioned "unicorn".

***

Blazing Swan is held in the middle of the wheat belt of Kulin, Western Australia, five hours from Perth. The theme for Blazing Swan 2014 was inception, marking their first event. Only a thousand tickets were being sold, which was a fraction of the 80,000 Burning Man attendees. The Unicorn Boudoir launched on the first day of the Blazing Swan. It was a platform to empower people to express themselves by wearing an outfit that disconnected them from the norm, something more confrontational than what they usually wore. It was all about embracing their inner charm. Everyone who left the boudoir became a unicorn who'd come out of a rainbow, as a piece of clothing could transform someone into a different personality.

"Thank you for the makeover! I am so happy!" said a man with a big belly who wore a tutu and necklace for the first time.

"I never thought I would wear something like this. Thanks, darling!" said a woman who was initially shy to wear a yellow sparkly costume because, as a lawyer, she was restrained by the formality at work.

Besides the unicorn clothing library, there were also horn-making and pasties workshops organised at the Unicorn Dome in preparation for the big day, the Unicorn March.

"Help yourself, babe! Choose your favourite colour and shape. You can find whatever you need here." Clara shimmied her pasties while showing craft materials such as duplexes, watercolours, glitter, glue guns, and fabrics.

I had put together my unicorn horn in advance, so I focused on the pasties making. In the beginning, I thought Camp Unicorn organised the making of baked pastries. But the pasties they referred to were the nipple tassels usually worn by female burlesque dancers to tease the audience. My skin tingled, knowing I was about to make something erotic, covering my nipples for other people's fantasies.

The big day finally came. The Camp Unicorn crew had already dressed up and put on their unicorn horns since the morning, too excited. The Unicorn March was an exercise in radical self-expression. This manifestation aimed to raise the awareness that unicorns are real, as are all of us. Many people hid from society, including me. The Unicorn March was the moment when we could shout and protest that we existed.

"Are you all ready to march?" Clara marshalled the crowd who were waiting outside the Unicorn Dome. "Repeat after me, 'We are real!'" she screamed into a megaphone.

"We are real!" the mass's voice followed.

I played a bongo drum as I walked beside Clara. My chin was up as I felt confident wearing a black under-bust corset that matched stripper tights and knee-high leather boots. A horn was attached to the forehead of my rainbow mohawk wig to top off the unicorn look. We marched around the Blazing Swan site, recruiting more people with unicorn horns to join us until we arrived at the horse ranch hundreds of metres from the tent area.

"You beautiful unicorns, you are going to run for your dream. It is not about who is the fastest! It is about releasing the magic within you!" Clara counted down for the unicorn race. "Ready, on 3, 2 and 1!"

We sprinted with a flare of joy as sunshine flooded our souls. The day's bliss led the Unicorn March from the ranch area to the salt lake. Our colourful outfits were beautiful in contrast to the white ground. The DJ diffused ambient electronic music from his booth, creating a dreamy atmosphere. The sound brought me to a girl wearing a giant unicorn headpiece, and I put my arms on her shoulders.

"Join us!" I beckoned the people.

The crowd followed, and it had converted into a long unicorn train within split seconds. I orchestrated a movement so everyone behind me could copy. I kicked first my left foot, then my right, and threw my arms from side to side. People at the back followed, and together we composed a spontaneous unicorn dance ritual to end the Unicorn March.

"Can I say that you are amazing? I had so much fun dancing at the end." A stranger with pink face paint and excessive glitter on her forehead approached me.

"You are such a sexy thing with that corset," another stranger with a gold unicorn horn said.

"I love you so much." Clara hugged me after the parade.

The people at Blazing Swan saw me as a person, as more than an Asian immigrant and a target of the *"No Asians"* statement on Grindr. On the salt lake, I stood and rotated 180 degrees while spreading my hands. I felt so blessed that I was in a welcoming and nurturing environment that helped me appreciate myself. The people in the Unicorn March had embraced my existence as a gift to them. So often, I felt like a lost soul and a weirdo. But when I finally found my tribe, I came to see that I am just imperfectly beautiful.

***

Most theme camps at Blazing Swan were created by community groups living in the suburb of Fremantle. Shiva Tea House offered a chill-out place and a variety of tea. People went there during the day to recover from a big night as they provided healing sessions using didgeridoos. Kamp Koasis was one of the biggest camps at Blazing Swan. They organised various workshops during the day and music entertainment with free brewed beer at night. They also hosted a Rum Punch event, where everybody dressed in pirate costumes to enjoy the free rum and live music. Everyone shared their gifts without expecting anything in return, exercising the act of giving.

Karina and Nadia, my best friends from Indonesia, who had just moved to Perth following a year-long working holiday visa, also came with me to Blazing Swan. We dedicated Kamp Koasis as a place to spend the nights out. On one stormy evening, the dance floor was packed shoulder to shoulder as people took refuge in the Kamp Koasis dome. The rain was getting heavier as we danced in front of the DJ's table. The lights and music suddenly went off, but it did not bother the crowd. They started clapping and dancing until the generator came back on. The party spirit eventually stopped when the dance floor started to flood. The DJ had to unplug the electricity while the Kamp Koasis crew covered the sound system with plastic to protect it from the water leaking off the roof. It was the beginning of chaos.

"What shall we do?" Karina looked at me.

"Let's help them." We went to the corner of the dome to hold up the bamboo columns, which had started cracking because of the heavy water accumulating on the tent's roof.

"One more time!" We pushed the water from the curved part of the tent so it flowed down onto the ground.

The situation worsened as the rain fell hard, and people started evacuating.

"Let's get out of here!" Karina screamed.

"How about staying in our car?" Nadia suggested.

"This is like a rescue mission from *Titanic!*" I joked as we ran, soaking wet.

Karina, Nadia and I had an intimate reunion inside the car. We belly-laughed over nostalgic party stories in Jakarta and reminisced over travelling to deserted places in Java. They had witnessed me evolve from a poor student surviving in a metropolitan city to a sparkling unicorn with a big horn. We all pictured our immigrant dreams in Australia, about their plans on the working holiday visa and my goal to get permanent residence status. The Land Down Under had united these three Indonesians in another adjoining adventure.

"I wondered if the effigy burn will still proceed tomorrow night with this kind of weather?" Nadia murmured.

The storm lasted for hours. We stayed in the car and kept munching on snacks while watching the drizzling rain with occasional thunder and lightning. You do not always need big moments to appreciate a friendship. Having a quiet time together without the pressure to fill in the dead air is remarkable too. There is no need for empty words to be comfortable with long-time friends. We let it be cosy.

***

The night after the storm was the peak moment of Blazing Swan. People gathered around the effigy an hour early to witness the burning of a twenty-metre-high swan. Safety ranger volunteers inspected the crowd barrier to ensure the burning procession would go without incident. They'd learned from Burning Man, where some spectators had run into the middle of the burning effigy because of the influence of drugs or suicidal acts.

The Fire Tribes were the opening act with performances of fire circus skills, accompanied by an African drumming circle. It was raining when the giant swan started to be burned, and it became spiritual as the element of fire intersected with water and wind. Seeing the burning effigy was like watching a flashback of memories; my emotions got switched on while watching the flames before my eyes.

I wished the fire had cleansed my bitter moments, like it was slowly eating the effigy. As the blaze grew, I hoped to let go of the unfinished business of my parents' expectations towards marriage, as I was still hiding my sexual orientation from them. My eyes welled with tears when I gazed at the left wing of the swan falling to the ground. I felt broken. The flame shuffled my flashback of endless nights searching for love, but it dumped me alone in a dark place. I prayed in front of the fire as if I had found a new god. I begged for love to appear in the right place, at the right time; and for the strength to continue the journey until I crossed paths with that soulmate.

The other wing of the swan plummeted, and I started another prayer. I asked for the strength to be gentle to myself and appreciate the things I did, even if I did not succeed. The flames reminded me of my own anger when I did not get what I wanted. I took a deep breath and closed my eyes as the drum sounds echoed. After watching the burning effigy for half an hour, I did not want to think about anything. I wanted an empty mind, just as the swan had turned to ashes. The effigy was burned, and the new spirit had awoken.

I felt reincarnated as I unlocked my inner unicorn. Like the Blazing Swan effigy, even the beautiful things could turn to ash. I should not fear radical self-expression because life is temporary.

There was a time when I had walked alone to explore myself. But finding a tribe could also be a part of the process of finding myself. I had received communal love through the Camp Unicorn tribe and the people at Blazing Swan. Their collective love was the foundation on which I would celebrate my existence.

Blazing Swan lit me up to keep walking on my path and passed me the best legacy I'd ever had. The corset and the pasties I wore from the boudoir and the unicorn character I found through Camp Unicorn were the inceptions of my journey as a burlesque performer. Somewhere on the west coast, the swan had been burnt, and a unicorn had been born.

16 THE PAGEANT

I am an immigrant who searches for freedom above a better life. Every aspect of life could get better, but it would mean nothing if the voice had been silenced, footsteps had been shackled, and the mind had been imprisoned. I found freedom in Australia, to be a proud gay man and magical unicorn. And I used those privileges to step onto the world stage in support of people who sought the light.

I felt empowered after attending Blazing Swan. My radical self-expression motivated me to look further for an opportunity to spread the unicorn spirit with a broader audience, especially the LGBTQIA+ community in Indonesia. I wanted to share that it is okay to be differently fabulous and to be the person we are destined to be. Even though it is not easy to discover freedom, I wished for them to know that they are not alone in their struggles.

I came across an article from LGBTQIA+ online news reporting on the Mr Gay World winner 2013. I never knew that the pageant existed. I investigated further and realised there had never been any representative from Indonesia since the pageant had started in 2009. That was when my random thought surfaced: I should participate in the Mr Gay World competition to underpin the initial mission of expanding my unicorn quintessence within the LGBTQIA+ community in Indonesia.

Oppression from hard-line Islamist groups had pushed LGBTQIA+ people in Indonesia to live under the radar. Before I moved to Australia, an Islamist group had terminated the 4th Conference of ILGA (International Lesbian, Gay, Bisexual, Trans and Intersex Association) Asia held in Surabaya. The Q! Film Festival, the first-ever LGBTQIA+ film festival organised in a predominantly Muslim country, was cancelled due to threats made by the infamous Front for the Defence of Islam (FPI). The resistance towards the LGBTQIA+ community in Indonesia made it important for minority groups to be visible to change prejudices. Somebody had to show Indonesian society that there are people like us in other parts of the world, coming from different races and professional backgrounds. Being gay is not a result of Western propaganda, as I had been taught by some Islamic preachers.

There were no age limitations on the candidates to join Mr Gay World competition, but most countries had a national selection process to choose their delegates. My option was to submit a wild card application designed for independent participants who did not have a national organisation, producer, or sponsor. It was a route for a single fighter applicant like me. My registration form was submitted to the Mr Gay World organisation within days. I backed it up with a blog link capturing my experience as a gay Asian man living in Australia.

"Note that you still have to organise the flight, visa application, and all the outfits by yourself." The National Director for Asia wrote an email to confirm that I had been accepted to represent Indonesia in Mr Gay World 2014 in Rome, Italy.

I announced on Facebook immediately, *"Let me introduce myself: The first representative from Indonesia at Mr Gay World!"*

The unicorn spirit made me feel unstoppable. I was not initially worried about the repercussions of my participation in Mr Gay World until my Indonesian colleague at work, an alumnus of Ocean Engineering, came to my desk.

"I am here not to judge because you are an adult. I am just worried about your safety because your participation is quite controversial."

"Eh? How did you get the news?" A soft and shaky voice came out of my mouth.

It turned out that one of my university friends on Facebook had taken a screenshot of my post and circulated it within the Ocean Engineering mailing group, consisting of students, alumni and lecturers. It had triggered a group discussion amongst my cohort to send a mediator to speak to me.

"Why do you want to participate in Mr Gay World?" My university friend, known for being very religious, messaged me. *"Don't you remember that once you were involved in our Islamic group? Please pray more and ask God for help,"* she added.

There was back-and-forth chatting with my old friends who tried to impede me from participating in the pageant. But I kept going. This was a test of the radical self-expression principle I'd found at Blazing Swan. I knew I had full support from my friends in Perth, which was enough for me.

"There will be gold wings coming out of your back, attached to a harness on your chest!" Goldy, who had introduced me to Camp Unicorn, helped me design the national costume. "It is inspired by *Garuda*." Goldy referred to the eagle, a national symbol of Indonesia.

"Consider this a gift. As a gay Jew, I can relate to your struggle of growing up in a religious society."

***

The Mr Gay World 2014 contestants stayed an hour out of Rome's city centre. Upon arrival, we gathered in a swimming pool area, and waited for the roommate arrangements. I greeted the delegates one by one as I was enthusiastic about meeting gay guys from all around the world.

"Give me a high five!" A contestant from Ireland became my roommate following the announcement by the organiser.

My excitement faded when I discovered how compact our room was. There were two single beds with half a metre between them and a single bathroom. It reminded me of a cabin. I'd expected the pageant to be luxurious, but I should have known from the beginning as the name of the accommodation complex said it all: Camping Village.

The first day was about sightseeing around Rome and visiting the Colosseum. Everything was enjoyable at the start, but the next day things escalated quickly. We went to the beach, where each contestant had the opportunity to get an official swimwear photoshoot. After the photo session, we returned to the bus to continue the subsequent activities.

"Sorry for the delay," the usher announced. "Apparently, one of the contestants has decided to stay at the beach with his boyfriend and does not want to return with you guys. He is too drunk!"

The rumour circulating said that his boyfriend had pushed him to quit out of jealousy that he was sharing a room with a hot contestant from a European country. He disappeared from the competition the following day without saying goodbye to us. The situation got more heated over the next few days because another contestant also decided to leave. He claimed to the judges that the pageant was poorly organised and he did not share common values with the organisation. Everyone was shocked; he was deemed to be one of the strong contenders to win the crown.

The competition continued as if nothing had happened until the in-depth interview day. Five judges from different backgrounds waited for me in the meeting room: a local politician, a journalist, LGBTQIA+ activists, and the head of the Mr Gay World organisation itself. I came to the judges' room wearing a green suit and trousers like I was celebrating St. Patrick's Day.

"What would you do if you won the Mr Gay World title?" the chairman of Mr Gay World asked me.

I took a deep breath to remain calm. "I would give my title to the runner-up."

The room went silent, and the judges froze.

"Are you insulting us?" A lesbian politician with an Italian accent raised her voice. "Why are you even here then?" She shrugged, palms up.

"People like me cannot win the title. I would be risking my life instead. Even participating in the competition as a wild card, I've already got unwelcome responses from some communities in Indonesia, including from the LGBTQIA+ community itself. I received a death threat before I arrived here." I raised my voice and gave her eye-to-eye contact as my self-defence mechanism.

"If you need to apply for asylum, let me know. I did that when I moved to the UK," said an LGBTQIA+ activist from Nigeria on the panel.

"I am working towards my Australian permanent residence visa." I tapped my foot on the floor to channel my nerves. "Besides, I just ignored the threat as it only occurred on social media. They were just strangers from a conservative Muslim background, using a Quran verse to justify killing gay people." I sighed.

"How conservative is Indonesia?" The Nigerian activist leaned towards me, trying to pay more attention to my answer.

"There were massive protests in different cities organised by radical Muslim organisations when Miss World 2013 was held in Indonesia. They demonstrated over a bikini session in the pageant, which was deemed against Islamic values.

"Participating in the pageant is already my effort to represent the Indonesian LGBTQIA+ community in front of an international audience, without creating a polemic in my home country. This is the beginning of my activism. I am gradually raising awareness about LGBTQIA+ rights in Indonesia to the world. I am standing up for myself here in Rome for that reason. However, I could not win the title because it would be too risky. I just hope more people will continue in my footsteps after I participate in Mr Gay World 2014."

"Wow, you just dropped a bomb. Your answer blew my mind." The journalist put his pen on the table.

I left the interview room feeling overwhelmed. I knew that some of the judges had not liked my answers based on their body language and the tone of their voices. But I had to keep going and be ready to appear on the final night's stage when the pageant would be broadcast internationally. I was hoping that some people in the LGBTQIA+ community in Indonesia would watch me and be inspired by my participation. That

The Pageant

was my unicorn's mission, carried all the way from Perth.

***

The Mr Gay World final was held in the Gay Village Rome and was attended by thousands of people. All the contestants started the show with an opening dance. When it finished, we sat on stage to see our video introductions on the big screen. The event continued with the first catwalk in formal dress.

"Mr Gay Indonesia, Ozak!" The host presented me.

I tried to walk as fiercely as possible, not even smiling because I did not know the difference between pageant and runway model catwalks. I remembered from the video tutorial on YouTube that my eyes had to speak louder than my body gestures during the catwalk. When I reached the front of the stage, I looked at the audience for a few seconds without blinking until my pupils were dry.

I switched my focus to the second catwalk for the casual outfit session, where I wore a psychedelic shirt that I'd bought from a second-hand shop. At the front of the stage, I did three seconds of shuffle dance as my final pose, and I could hear the audience clapping.

"One, two, three, four, five…" Backstage, all the participants did push-ups, hoping the muscles would pop up before returning to the stage for the swimsuit catwalk.

It was the first time in my life wearing swimming trunks and showing my body to a big crowd. Whatever happened on the stage, I kept telling myself to suck in my belly and squeeze my abs while pretending I was smiling from the heart.

While the judges were discussing the top ten, the contestants completed a sports challenge. We were divided into groups of four and performed cross-fit movements, as demonstrated by a fitness instructor.

"Congratulations to group five!" The host referred to my group, which consisted of participants from India, Iceland and Hong Kong. We won the sports challenge, as we were the fastest and had the most correct technique.

"Everybody has to vote by giving a rose to the person they think most deserves the congeniality title." The host explained the next award.

The delegate from India won Mr Congeniality. A well-deserved award because he is a celebrity back home and had been so entertaining during our time at the lodge.

"Please welcome our boy band of the night!" The host continued with the talent show, where some contestants sang, danced and acted.

I was looking forward to showcasing my voice. However, it was challenging to find the spotlight when I had to perform "I Want It That Way" by the Backstreet Boys with seven other contestants. I did not sing the solo part in the refrain. The vocal coach had asked me to sing the tenor section as he knew I could harmonise the song. I felt robbed when I witnessed one of the contestants sing out of tune. I knew I could have done it better. But I let my spotlight fade away.

After the talent show finished, all the contestants gathered on the stage wearing formal attire again. It was time for the host to announce the top ten.

"And the last spot goes to Venezuela!" The host wrapped up the announcement.

I kept smiling at the audience, despite not hearing my name. I consoled myself it must be because of the things I'd said in the in-depth interview. However, seeing the euphoria of the contestants whose names were called made me jealous. I sat backstage and felt disappointed to be an observer in the competition, not an achiever. I realized that I had been too confrontational with the judges. I could have pretended I wanted the title when they'd asked me about it. If I were in the top ten, people would have noticed more of the Indonesian delegate, and that would have given me more visibility.

I became emotional at the end of the final night. I felt alone after the celebration of Mr Gay World 2014, won by Mr Gay UK. Every contestant had their producer and team to congratulate them. Some of their boyfriends had flown across the world to support them in person. I felt like nobody cared that I was there. I dove onto the dance floor and ordered four rounds of vodka mixed with energy drinks without a break in between to cure my disappointment.

"Do you want to come to my place?" A local who made out with me on the dance floor grabbed the back of my neck.

"Oh, no! I have to pack my outfits." I stepped backwards.

I rushed backstage to collect my stuff as I remembered the bus would transport us back to our accommodation, but the alcohol started kicking in. I rarely drink much liquor in a short period. As a result, my heart started to beat fast, and my head was spinning. I sat down when I finally found other contestants. My eyes were closed, and my body could not move. Everything felt so heavy.

"Ozak, can you hear me?" I was listening, but I could not respond to anyone.

I tried to control my breath, but my heart was pumping like a drum roll because of the energy drink.

"Open your mouth!" The Northern Ireland delegate who

worked as a nurse forced me to drink water to sober me up.

Water spilt out of my mouth while I tried to swallow some of it to gain consciousness from dehydration. Once I started to function again, I drank two litres of water immediately as I was scared of alcohol poisoning. I could stand up after half an hour and crawl to the toilet, only to vomit while the contestants were watching me. I became one of those people who embarrassed themselves by drinking out of control.

"Let me walk you to the shuttle bus." A delegate from Spain sent me back to the lodge.

I got to my room and went to the toilet to vomit again. While other participants were celebrating the last night together, I cried in the shower as I could not handle the catastrophe of the final night.

I sat in the bathroom corner for a long time while the hot water poured over my body. I was like a Roman sculpture; naked and rugged, unconcerned with vanity.

17 THE VISA

There is something about sad endings. The memories lingered at the back of my mind while the clock kept ticking and dragging my fragile emotions into the daily routine. Like the last scene of the Mr Gay World competition, I tried to cover it up with smiley photos on social media. I let my friends see only my bright side. Days and weeks passed. Those recollections dissolved over time until I received a private message on Facebook from my older brother a few months later.

"*Ozak, I saw on the internet that you joined Mr Gay World. That is your call. However, I need to remind you that we still have parents. You also know what our religion and culture look like. We are all proud that you work in Australia. But you should think in advance about what you do in the future because Mum and Dad always check on you. With the internet these days, we cannot hide things. Even our neighbour sometimes sees you on YouTube!*"

"*Amen,*" I replied.

If I was to come out, I would do it all out. And I did it. I'd come out not only to friends and family but to the world as Mr Gay Indonesia. My parents had not commented yet on my participation, but they still sent me an occasional reminder message to keep praying five times a day as a Muslim. They did not know how to approach the situation, unlike my brother, who had found out online. But that was exactly my intention: to minimise direct confrontation and for them to take their time to digest the information before contacting me. That was why my mother had always tidied up my room and secretly read my diaries in my teenage years; our communication had always been based on written clues, not impulsive conversation.

My job was to make my family notice, and it was not my responsibility for them to accept me. It had taken a whole new adventure in Australia for me to be content with my sexual orientation. Therefore, I did not expect them to understand my life path. One thing is for sure, the distance between Indonesia and Australia helped reduce the repercussions of my participation in Mr Gay World. There was no drama like when my parents discovered my cousin's topless male collage pictures. Far away across the Indian Ocean, I could live life in my own way.

The repercussion that concerned me was when I visited Indonesia to gather documents for my permanent residence visa application. I was afraid of what would happen once I arrived at the immigration checkpoint at Soekarno Hatta International Airport. Would I be forbidden to enter my country or, worse, get arrested for defamation after representing Indonesia in the Mr Gay World? The reality was, I passed the border control without any issues. The immigration officer stamped my passport and did not say a word. It turned out my involvement was not as controversial as I had thought. The public was too busy following Indonesia's presidential election at the time.

But just because I'd passed immigration did not mean that my worries would stop. I had a few months to go to be eligible for my Australian permanent residence visa application. Of all the required documents I had to provide, the Indonesian police clearance was the hardest to get. The Indonesian Embassy in Australia did not offer this service. It had to be submitted in person to the Indonesian Police Institute.

"It is only valid for one year, and you must reapply from the beginning." The officer returned my old police clearance and did not care that I had already flown from Australia. "Collect recommendation letters from where you live to verify that you have no criminal record!"

I did not want to fail at processing my visa due to one of the documents being stuck at the bottom of the administration valley. I promised myself it would be the last hassle dealing with Indonesian bureaucracy. After five days of going back and forth between the local police stations and government institutions, I finally received the police clearance that had cost me an international flight to process. Perhaps the journey was not about getting the piece of a paper, but about the final test that brought me closer to my Australian dream.

***

Waiting is part of the immigration master plan. That was the challenge I faced in counting down to the day when I would be eligible to apply for a permanent residence visa. It had been such a long ride since I'd joined my company as a graduate engineer. I'd passed the probation stage and had ascended from the bottom of the employee grade to become a Project Engineer. I'd tasted the glorious feeling of my first promotion letter and the temporary working visa sponsored by my company. Everything had gone according to plan—until the nightmare came.

It was the middle of 2015 when the oil and gas crisis started.

There was one word that could jeopardise everything: redundancy. If it had happened, all my efforts to successfully gather the required documents, including the Indonesian police clearance, would have been a waste. Redundancy meant a catastrophe because I would have to find another company within ninety days to sponsor me for a working visa again, and wait another two years to become eligible for a permanent residence visa. My task was crystal clear; I had to avoid redundancy at all costs.

Tough times teach people how to survive. My survival mechanism was to prove I was a money-maker for the company. Many clients wanted to execute their projects quickly to reduce their budgets. I optimised my work approach and automated as many calculation sheets as possible to cut analysis time. Projects that would typically take months to finish, I could now wrap up within a couple of weeks. I suppressed the work stress by reminding myself how close I was to my immigration goal. The only way to create a safety net was to make the clients and my boss happy.

"Thank you everyone for coming to this Monday morning meeting." My engineering manager, Jonathan, stood before our team to address the recession. "Management has decided to transfer two engineers from Perth to the Houston office to avoid redundancy in our department." He walked back and forth as he gathered the words. "I do not want to decide. Please discuss this matter amongst yourselves. Your voluntary decision will help us all."

The room was silent. The meeting shocked everyone, and it left me in an uncomfortable position. I was the most suitable candidate for the transfer, given I was single and did not own property in Perth. But I was so close to reaching my Australian dream.

"I cannot move to the USA. I want to apply for a permanent residence visa here." I talked to some of my colleagues to give them an understanding of my circumstances.

The office atmosphere proliferated speculations about who would take the hot seats. Everyone had discreet conversations. But in the end, somebody had to do it on behalf of the team. My two co-workers voluntarily accepted the transfer offer two weeks after the meeting. Both had new babies and preferred to be transferred to Houston rather than lose their job. It was easier for them as they already had Australian permanent residency status.

Losing two engineers in the Perth office was only a temporary solution for a few months. The company's top management still pressured my engineering manager to let go of more staff.

"I know it has been a tough few months, and I'm trying my best not to make anyone redundant. Therefore, I kindly ask you to take an unpaid holiday to reduce company costs. It will help our cash flow for a while." Jonathan lowered his voice to end the speech during the second budget cut meeting.

The crisis brought the team to be closer than before. We showed up to work knowing that everyone was fragile, and shared our insecurities with each other. One morning, I arrived at the office to read an announcement regarding the organisation's restructuring.

"This cannot be right!" I was speechless that my engineering manager was the one who had been let go first while he had tried his best to keep all of us in the company.

Because of the new structure, some senior consultants and engineers decided to take voluntary redundancy. There was the smell of politics behind the curtain, but I kept quiet because I was insecure in my position. Watching my department shrink due to the crisis was heart-wrenching. We used to be close and knew each other well. The atmosphere of work had utterly changed. The cubical area became empty. Every day, people wondered if they would become the next victim to get laid off. I came to the office like a convict awaiting execution.

The permanent residence visa is a labyrinth. The government adjusts the rules every year to tighten the requirements. A permanent resident has privileges similar to the Australian citizen, except they cannot vote in elections. I had devoted two years to holding a 457 Working Visa before becoming eligible to apply for company sponsorship. This route was already the shortcut compared to the Points-tested Skilled Independent Visa or Partner Visa. But being eligible was not the final hurdle. My company had to sponsor me with the intention of maintaining my employment contract for a further two years. It was a huge request amid the crisis.

"I understand the recession is still ongoing. But as of today, I am eligible to apply for a permanent residence visa, and I wonder if the company can sponsor me?" I spoke to the Human Resources manager in her office.

"Your colleague asked the same thing recently. But I didn't give him a definite answer as he might be made redundant." She lowered her voice.

"Oh, really?" I forced a smile, thinking about my fate.

"But don't you worry! I know your name is not on the list of people who might get laid off." She leaned towards me.

"Okay, I won't tell anyone." I crossed my fingers under the table.

"Our migration agent will process the employee's nomination paperwork as the main document required for your application. But you also need to understand that the company cannot pay for the visa cost."

"I am more than happy to cover all the expenses. But what do you mean by nomination paperwork?"

"That is a crucial step to prove you have the necessary skills as an engineer in your field. Without the nomination paperwork, you'd have to go through a skill assessment organised by Engineers Australia, which could take more than a year."

"That sounds complicated!" I bit my lip.

"You'll be fine! You've already proven your capability as an engineer by having at least two years of working experience in our company."

"Can I please get in touch with the migration agent?"

"Yes, they are very accommodating. The agent understands how to mitigate the risk of the visa being rejected. You know, in the case of the skilled worker nominated position being filled, unsatisfactory medical check-up results, or losing the job during the visa process." She gave me the migration agent's details.

"How much is the fee?" I looked at the business card.

"I think it is around $7,000 per person for the migration agent service and visa application cost. And it is not refundable if the outcome is unsuccessful." Her eyes focused on the computer screen to double-check the information.

***

Waiting for the permanent residence visa application update was like watching the night sky for a shooting star. Every day my brain wondered about the outcome amid uncertainty. Within my circle of friends, I had seen how a visa could affect life's direction. Some of them had left Australia as they could not secure permanent residency, even though they'd studied in Australia for a decade. Some had fallen in love with Australia while on their working holiday visa but could not extend their stay, as finding a company to sponsor them was one in a million. Some decided to marry an Australian when love was the only way to secure their legality in a foreign country. A visa is a form of future destiny.

"Good morning! Ozak speaking." I went to the meeting room for some privacy to answer a call from an unknown number.

"This is Julia, the immigration agent."

"Hi, Julia! Glad to speak to you again." I closed the door and leaned against the wall.

"Regarding your visa…" She paused. "I'm calling to let you know that your permanent residence visa has been granted!" She waited for my response, like a phone call from a reality show offering a jackpot prize.

"What? Oh my god!" My jaw dropped. Within seconds, every cell in my body responded to my excitement. It tingled and gave me goosebumps. The invisible immigrant burden on my shoulders was lifted that morning. The news flashed before my eyes like I had finally caught a shooting star four months after the visa submission. It was the second happiest phone call I'd ever had in my life, after the job offer. It gave me the verdict to live in Australia permanently, finding and re-defining my home at last.

"*Permanent Residence Visa has been granted!*" I updated my Facebook status to express my feelings, as I could not scream out loud in my quiet office.

That exciting news led me to a long stroll around the city centre during my coffee break. Every footstep was like a rewind to when I'd arrived in Perth, alone. I thanked myself for surviving the workload of every day, and for spending time on the weekend to ensure the computer analyses ran well. I thanked myself for learning English by listening to conversations in different accents, writing reports with lots of editing, and feeling occasional loneliness in my cubicle as I spent the whole day sitting behind the desk. I thanked myself for conquering my poor self-esteem at the office because I only held a bachelor's degree from Indonesia, unlike my colleagues with PhD titles. I thanked myself for taking the first step three years ago, showing up at the office with a door-to-door job application, which had flipped my destiny coin to the victorious side.

The phone call was a shred of evidence that I had subdued my fear of being made redundant during the oil and gas crisis. It was a nerve-racking odyssey, but I thanked myself for defeating every obstacle and finally reaching my immigration goal. My one-way ticket to Australia had turned out to be a solid permanent landing.

18 THE COSTUMES

"Congrats on getting your permanent residence visa!" Jihan, my fake girlfriend, called me.

"Finally!" I exhaled a big sigh.

"I am so happy for you! You can be a fabulous unicorn there! It's not safe here, you know. Indonesia is going backwards!" Her voice blasted through my phone speaker.

The face of Indonesia in 2015 was conservative. The country's slogan, "Unity in Diversity", seemed only applicable to majority groups. Aceh province introduced caning punishment for anyone caught having same-sex relations following their Sharia Law implementation. Censorship on television became more stringent after the national commission censored the *kebaya*, a traditional Indonesian women's outfit, as it showed cleavage. Condom distribution was banned in mini-markets in some provinces, as it was deemed to promote sex outside marriage.

There was such a disparity between what was happening in Indonesia and what was happening across the sea. The privilege of living in Australia as an openly gay man and permanent resident provoked me to delve further into my new identity. I was in a conducive environment to manifest creativity, unafraid of social and religious prejudice. While Indonesia gradually became more conservative, I went in the opposite direction. I became more explorative of radical self-expression through the outfits I wore.

The habit of dressing up in costumes initially came from the people in the Blazing Swan community. My wardrobe had evolved into two sections: daily attire and party outfits. At a Halloween party, I wore an under-bust corset to embrace my pectoral muscles. At a New Year's Eve party, I put on a mankini to be proud of my bulge. At a friend's pool party, I covered my entire body with gold glitter to make my skin shine. If there was no specific dress code, I would wear leggings in various colours to welcome my arse curve.

Every time I read news of the religious oppression back in Indonesia, it fuelled me to dig more into the habit of dressing up. Growing up as a Muslim, there was an inner rebellion to break away from the religious dogma of my past. Dressing up was a way for me to challenge the Islamic norm which had been ingrained in me since childhood. I learned how to own my body through the costumes I put on from one party to the next. Every outfit taught me to be comfortable with my shape. I found the freedom to express my sexuality and enjoy the sensuality of a piece of clothing. The more I wore different costumes, the gentler I became with my skin. I told myself it was okay to be sexy. I should not be shy about my artistry and energy.

***

The costume is a kind of branding. My colleagues identified me as creative as I always dressed up at the annual company event. The costume is a manner of communication; there are stories behind what people wear. It can be a stimulant to break down the barriers with strangers and befriend them at house parties. The costume is a wave frequency. People exchange their warm smiles as a compliment whenever I walk on the street in fabulous clothing.

"Nice outfit, darling!" Sometimes strangers politely asked for impromptu photos and mentioned me on social media.

But the things that most shaped my attitude and boldness came from the bad experiences. One night, I stayed over at a friend's place and left the apartment wearing Hello Kitty shorts and a sparkly maroon jacket. It was my outfit of choice to attend an art show. What I wore did not please a random guy in the apartment complex when he saw me walking on the ground floor.

"Oi, faggot!" he screamed from his balcony. "Look what you're wearing, faggot!" He was shouting louder than before.

I froze for a second, digesting what to do next. The easiest option was to yell back at him. I was in an apartment complex where every unit was connected to each other. A brawl could easily attract attention from other neighbours, and there could be a great fight scene between the faggot and the ignorant. But after I assessed the situation in a couple of seconds of left-brain thinking, I chose to ignore him. I did not want that stranger attacking my friend's flat when I'd gone. I chose to ghost him. He was invisible to me.

Being silent and not making eye contact with strangers was my default manner whenever I dressed up in public. It was a self-defence mechanism not to engage people's attention. One Saturday night, Goldy from Camp Unicorn and I left the gay club wearing devil and angel costumes. As we walked down the street to find a cab, a group of people ridiculed us.

"You should be ashamed of what you're wearing," a woman yelled.

"It is who I am! Shame on you!" Goldy pointed a finger at her.

"You're a man! Why are you wearing a wig?" she laughed.

"Mind your own business, girl!" said Goldy as we walked further away from them.

That incident gave me deep thoughts. Perhaps Goldy had dared to talk back because they had heard so much hate speech that they'd had enough of being treated that way. Maybe my muted response to bigotry would also have a limit at some point, as the pain that comes from hate speech does not just disappear. Sometimes, it leaves a mark and accumulates.

Some people have different interpretations of costumes. There were times when I wore leggings to be comfortable with my curves, and then my arse would get slapped without consent by strangers. I remember someone slapped me from behind at a music festival. When I looked back, a group of teenagers giggled while avoiding eye contact. A few seconds later, one of them tried to slap me again. I caught her hand as I turned quickly, and she just smiled. She thought it was funny for a guy to wear leggings. She could not accept that I wore leggings for myself, not as a joke.

"Consent means always choosing to respect others' boundaries. No one should touch you without permission." Clara from Camp Unicorn comforted me.

After discussing consent, I understood that I got to decide about my own body. I started to tell strangers that it was not okay to randomly slap my arse without consent, and it was worse if it was considered ridicule. But I was not always in the mood to explain it, and people sometimes did not bother with words. That was when I would slap back as revenge. Blood paid for with blood—that was how I treated the unsolicited slap. Those people would walk away and leave my arse alone when they recognised that it had become a confrontation.

Wearing a raunchy costume, for me, is about breaking down stereotypes. From my experience of attending parties, I learned that some strangers expected me to be shy and quiet because I am Asian. "You're hot for an Asian man." Often, I'd get that comment when I revealed my skin and body. I was unaware of what people thought about Asian men until I learnt they considered me an anomaly.

Public transport was my battlefield when I wore an eccentric outfit. I liked to listen to techno-house music through headphones and walk down the train station corridor as if it was the runway at a fashion show. I walked to the beat of the music and looked at a single point in front of my eyes. In my head, I was fierce. I had to be that way because there was always a risk of getting abused by random people on the street.

The costume taught me to become a bold person. I learned how to control my nerves when I walked in busy places. However, I spent many nights walking on the road holding a key between my fingers in self-defence mode. There were competing feelings within me, wanting to practice self-expression versus wishing to remain safe. Every time I took off my costumes in the bedroom, I became more compassionate to myself because I could see how fragile I was walking in the middle of a wild nightlife area in Perth. I knew my outfit should not worry me. Like everyone else who went for a night out, I just wanted to return home safely at the end of my evening, regardless of what I wore.

***

My costumes infused energy inside me to entertain people whenever I went to house parties. I was doing impromptu shows long before I discovered the burlesque scene and performed on stage. The first time I gave a lap dance was when I went to a David Bowie theme party for a friend's farewell.

"Yeah, baby! You like it, don't you?" I danced and forced my friend to eat a banana covered with thick chocolate spread.

There was a girl who joined me in the lap dance too. We both improvised by lying on the floor and putting our legs between each other like scissors until I broke her thumb as I pushed her legs too hard. Meanwhile, the chocolate spread became a hit at the party. Some guests started covering their nipples with it and licking each other.

I showed up at another party with a sexy scientist theme, wearing white stockings, a harness and a second-hand laboratory jacket. There was a three-metre-high swing installed in the house's backyard. My entertaining soul summoned me. I swung in front of the crowd as if performing circus movements, followed by a dance improvisation with my hand and foot in the air.

One of the guests came up to me after that. "Do you want to play with a hula hoop?"

We ended up creating a spontaneous hula hoop drinking game to see who could keep it going for the longest. People circled us, raising their beer bottles while shouting, "Woop! Woop! Woop!" My character that night had brought the party to life.

When Camp Unicorn organised a fundraising party, I volunteered to perform a lap dance as a raffle ticket price. I walked into the middle of the crowd wearing a kinky leather jockstrap and a head harness. I pulled the guy who won the raffle onto the dance floor and tied him to a chair while the audience watched us in a circle formation. I removed my head harness and put it on him to control his movement.

I took out a jar of chocolate spread and banana, the gimmick I'd used at the previous party. The raffle ticket winner whispered some English words when I was about to feed him. I paused as I did not understand what he said, and the crowd was noisy. I assumed he did not like the taste of it, so I moved on to the next trick. I continued the lap dance and grabbed the whipped cream. I sprayed it into my chest and asked him to lick it. The same thing happened; he did not want to eat it. In the end, I just kept grinding until the song finished.

"Thank you for the lap dance," he told me as I untied the harness.

"You did not like the chocolate and whipped cream?" I rested my hand on his right shoulder.

"I am lactose intolerant. I can't eat dairy products." He slowed down his words.

"Oh, sorry for the language barrier! I did not understand what it meant before." I hugged him as a gesture of my apology.

My confidence rose from one piece of costume to another. After a while, it made me realise that I needed a bigger platform with which to channel my creativity and self-expression. Then my friend Lisa approached me in the middle of the dance floor at a silent disco party.

"I think you should join the boylesque competition." Lisa paused her dance moves.

"What's boylesque?" I looked at her.

"It's a burlesque performance for males. You know burlesque, right?" She raised her right eyebrow.

"No, I don't." I shook my head.

"It's the art of teasing. What you have been doing at most house parties, basically." She poked me.

"What? Like dressing up, dancing, and taking off my clothes?" I showed her my nipple.

"Yes! Exactly, darling! Just do your thing, and you will be fine." She did a body roll movement while speaking.

"I do like taking off my clothes, indeed." I copied her body roll to tease her.

"Let me introduce you to my burlesque friend next time!" She continued to dance and grabbed my hands, pulling them into the air.

19 THE BOYLESQUE

"It is the art of teasing," Lisa said to me. "It is about suspense, expression, seduction and embracing body positivity."

Burlesque was a new term for my ears as no Indonesian word describes it. The closest illustration would be a striptease, which is taboo for Indonesians. People in Western countries consider burlesque an art form, whereas in a conservative country like Indonesia, people would see it as pornography.

Watching burlesque shows online was my first leap into the performance world. The first thing that captivated me was the diversity in the body shapes of the burlesque artists. It shattered the preconception that I had to have the fitness magazine cover look in order to perform. Burlesque is not just about being almost naked on stage but also about presenting our skin as performance art. It is a platform on which to serve a life experience on one platter: a mixture of teasing, music, costume, storytelling and stage production.

My boylesque journey started when I picked my stage name Tess OZteron, inspired by the testosterone hormone, which plays a vital role in the muscle strength of the male body. It was a prayer for my alter-ego to be wild and aggressive when performing on stage. I adopted a unicorn as my stage persona because I was already a devotee of Camp Unicorn. The unicorn protected me from being labelled as a sinner just because I am gay. The unicorn façade is also my shield against racism towards Asian immigrants. The unicorn is an umbrella for everything I want to be, considering the intersections between my religion, sexual orientation and race identities.

Tess OZteron was presented for the first time when I emailed the burlesque producer. I signed up for the competition without having any previous burlesque performance history or existing act to present. But I had creative experiences to back up my application.

"I participated in Mr Gay World 2014. I have experience in dancing, singing and strutting on the international stage.

I am involved in the Blazing Swan as part of Camp Unicorn, where I often dress up and do spontaneous lap dances. I also performed cabaret and theatre at school back in Indonesia.

My motivation to join the competition is not only to elevate my radical self-expression but also to let everyone know that unicorns do exist."

My application got accepted within a few weeks. The producer granted a newbie performer like me a chance to compete in their show. It was a serendipitous shot that allowed my unicorn alter-ego to finally emerge.

I had approximately five months to brew a five-minute premiere performance before showcasing it in a theatre with a thousand-seat capacity.

There were days I daydreamed about the performance ideas while pretending to read a project report at work. After a deep-rooted brainstorming, I created "The Birth of the Unicorn" to capture that, regardless of sexual orientation, religion and race, no one should have to hide who they truly are. My performance vision blended narration about unicorn empowerment with musical instruments, comedy dialogue, a sexy beat and a twist at the end.

My monthly salary became a saviour in procuring the unicorn costumes because I did not have the skills to create them from scratch. Neon pink dominated my outfits from head to toe, giving polarity to the testosterone muscle image, and harking back to the Pink Power Ranger of my childhood. The unicorn headpiece came all the way from the Netherlands and was designed by a costume maker who previously worked for Lady Gaga. It was specially customised, with a layer of pink glitter on the surface and rainbow hair at the back, that had cost me almost a thousand euros.

Online shops provided the rest of the costume, including high-heeled boots, a corset, brief lingerie, a robe and cock pouch. LED finger lights and two fibre-optic whips were added to the international shipping lists from the USA. Some items required signature upon delivery, and nobody was at my house during business hours. I always told the seller not to put product details on the package as it would be delivered to the office. I had to keep it all discreet to protect my career as an engineer. They were too hot to handle in a workplace environment.

"You got this massive box, but it's so light," said the receptionist in the lobby. "What is it?"

"Thank you for signing for the delivery. It is just a home decoration," I lied. It was the unicorn headpiece made from Styrofoam that I had been waiting for.

The pieces of the costume arrived one by one, and I would take selfies to see how they looked on my body. The mirror became my sparring partner to practise facial expressions while stripping off the outfits. Lipstick stains marked the glass surface from numerous attempts at conjuring up a feeling of seduction. My bedroom evolved into a mini dance studio whenever I found new choreography that matched the music. There were nights that I danced with the lights off using the two LED whips. "The Birth of the Unicorn" was made in the dark.

"Be careful! Those heels are so high!" My housemate bit her thumbs, worried I would fall when I walked around the house in eight-inch high-heeled boots.

The dance studio welcomed me for a two-hour hire the night before the competition. It was the first time I'd rehearsed the performance repetitively from beginning to end. I'd thought practising in my bedroom every night was enough, but soon I realised that I'd underestimated the difficulty of my outfits. The stage blocking was harder to execute with the heels on, and the unicorn headpiece made breathing difficult after a while. My confidence started to crumble as I was afraid of messing up the choreography at the competition. One night before my debut, I began to question my decision to compete. But there was no turning back; the unicorn had to arise and conquer the stage for the first time.

***

"So packed here!" I went backstage to a small dressing room shared between 20 female and male contestants on the night of the competition.

"I have a lot of costumes to wear for the classic, neo and unique performance categories!" a female burlesque artist commented. "Hence, I bring my own portable clothes rack."

"Luckily, boylesque participants only need to perform a single act." I exhaled.

The music and audience reaction travelled to the dressing room each time a performer went onstage. There were seven boylesque contenders, and I was performing towards the end, saving the unicorn for the last. Time went slowly backstage. I played my music over and over again while remembering the choreography. My nervousness did not get under my skin. I'd experienced far worse situations walking on the street while dressing up. Performing in the theatre was an upgrade from the underground house parties I used to go to. I was a stray unicorn among Persian cats, ready to cover the stage with rainbow poo.

"There is no other way to describe Tess OZteron, except he is a unicorn. He likes to lick rainbow ice cream and big-long horns. He is fed up knowing a cat can attract a million viewers on YouTube. Therefore, he has decided to come out tonight to show everyone that he is REAL!" the host introduced me.

The lights were switched off. Everyone fell silent as I came up to the stage, holding a white piece of fabric in the darkness to cover my whole body. The lighting shone towards me, creating a silhouette in the centre of the stage. I suspended the audience's enthusiasm. They could only see the shadow while listening to a narration about how powerful and invincible the unicorns were. When it finished, I ripped the fabric in half.

"Yay!" People screamed at my pink unicorn as the stage lights came back on.

I turned on the LED finger lights and moved my arms, following the music's rhythm. I was enjoying the initial part of the choreography until my heel got stuck in the back of my pink robe. "Damn!"

I tried to untangle it by lifting my feet, but the heel was too sharp. Within seconds, I improvised the dance choreography by bending my knee even lower to quickly use my hand to pull the robe out from underneath the heel. "Thank God!"

The choreography continued until I finally took off my headpiece as the music changed. The fresh air caressed my face. I could finally breathe freely and show facial expressions to the audience while lip-syncing the dialogue.

"Let's test your knowledge and see what you have learnt so far," as the lyrics played. "What colour is the unicorn?" I asked the audience while lip-syncing.

"Pink!" The crowd responded.

"Where are they dancing?" I continued.

"Rainbow!" The noise level was doubled.

"Please use one word to describe the texture of their magical fur." I made eye contact with the audience.

"Fluffyyyyy!" they all shouted.

"Smile! Yeah!" The dialogue stopped.

I evolved from a funny and playful character into sassy and sexy energy when the song transitioned to "Get Your Freak On" by Missy Elliott. The crowd cheered as I slowly removed my robe, revealing a pink bikini. I walked to the front of the stage and picked up the LED whips that changed colour every second. At that moment, my alter-ego possessed me. I felt sexy and liberated on the dance floor. As I was preparing for the final cue of my act, I lay down to grab the unicorn headpiece and raise it into the air. I took off the horn with my right hand and stuck it against my ass when the music ended with the phrase "Fuck Me". The lights turned off. The audience laughed out loud to see a detached horn being used as a sharp dildo.

Lisa came up to me during the break. "Congratulations on your performance! It was just, wow! I think you're the clear winner tonight!"

"You are too kind!" I patted her shoulder fur.

"Did you notice that you were the only Asian participant?" she added.

I received compliments from the audience during the intermission. They congratulated me on my performance as if I had already won the title. Some of them expressed their happiness, and we took photos together. I felt like a celebrity as my confidence level rose. More than that, I'd achieved the unicorn mission of representing a minority group in the competition.

I went backstage after the female burlesque contestants had finished their last performance category. We all did a group hug while waiting for the host to announce the winner. Deep down, I was worried about my ending, which I knew some people might find a bit vulgar. I remembered the initial conversation with the producer during the competition registration: "Your ending is a bit unusual. It will all depend on the judges' interpretation."

When I did not hear my name announced in the runner-up position, I was so hopeful that it would be me who won the title of Mr Boylesque Western Australia 2015. My expectations skyrocketed before the winner's announcement. In a split second, I was free-falling when the host finally announced someone else's name. My imagination bubbles delivering a winning speech had burst. The crown was not for me, and I kept the broken unicorn horn as it was.

"Congratulations guys!" I hid my disappointment in front

of the winners before I went backstage to pack up my costume.

I'd thought that night I could be like Napoleon, who came, saw and conquered.

Outside, Lisa hugged me and tried to cheer me up because I was not talking much. "Come here, darling. You did well!"

***

As a new performer, my ego told me I deserved to be a winner. I was still craving the crown when I watched the performance videos a few weeks later. My inner positive unicorn spirit had vanished after the competition because the result reminded me of my previous failure when I did not make it to the top ten at Mr Gay World 2014. It got worse as I let my thoughts do the self-blaming for the things I should have done—doing studio rehearsal more often, for example. I'd underestimated how challenging the boylesque competition was; each judge had different tastes and interpretations.

Nevertheless, I believed that I should keep going and reach for a bigger goal to prove that the unicorn was unstoppable. I researched online for international burlesque events and came across the Vienna Boylesque Festival. I looked at the previous year's performance and got more excited when I discovered that Conchita Wurst, the winner of Eurovision 2014, had performed on the opening night. Their website mentioned that the festival's vision was to create a burlesque family that went beyond just an annual event.

"You cannot do it because you are a newcomer, and your main goal should be to get paid at a local gig first," one of Perth's burlesque artists told me when I tried to discuss my intention one weekend at the local bar. "There have been Australian boylesque performers in the international festival. But they'd already won the national competition before they performed internationally." She sipped her Martini after preaching to me.

I finished a glass of gin and tonic in one attempt to calm myself down. I had not expected to have someone tell me that I could not achieve my goal just because I did not have a winning title. It was supposed to be a friendly catch-up to share my aspirations as a new performer. I was not there seeking her approval. Even if the dream seems wild, let one dream.

It was four months from the submission closing date for the Vienna Boylesque Festival. I fast-tracked my performance experience by taking many unpaid gigs in Perth and Melbourne, from Halloween to New Year's Parties. Any footage of Tess OZteron on the stage would add to my portfolio. My intention was lucid. I wanted to make a positive impression on my application for the Vienna Boylesque Festival.

"Since Thursday, we have been watching all the videos and are not even close to halfway through the submitted applications. That means lots of coffee and/or bubbly to shimmy our way through to the very last application – looooong weekend ahead!

Again, a big thank you to all of you lovely performers – who are the essence of the festival. Much love, VBF Family."

Every day I visited their Facebook page, hoping to get an update on my application. Two weeks after the submission date, I received an email titled *"Va Va Voom!"* I'd just woken up. My eyes were barely open, but I already held my mobile phone while curling under the blanket.

"Dear Tess OZteron! Yass! You know damn well how to VA-VA-VOOM!" I changed the phone screen display to a brighter level. I did not want to miss any sentences in the email.

"We are really thrilled by your submission..." I focused on

reading the last paragraph and hoped I would not find the word "but" or "regret".

"Therefore, we would love for you to perform at the Vienna Boylesque Festival 2016. Please send us a confirmation email within two weeks if you would like to accept our offer."

20 THE INTERNATIONAL DEBUT

Vienna was calling in the midst of chaos as the oil and gas crisis worsened in 2016. My company had laid off numerous employees, and those who had survived had been asked to take time off. I made the most of it by taking two months of unpaid leave to execute my international debut during the European spring season. Focusing on my life experiences was all it took to not worry about the risks of being made redundant.

Rome was my first stop. To expand my network, I contacted Fabrizio, a local performer who would also be performing at the Vienna Boylesque Festival. He shared his experience in the burlesque scene at a coffee shop.

"I am an idealist. I started researching burlesque history before I decided to perform," he said while smoking a cigarette. "I even flew to Spain just to learn Flamenco. I showcased my matador burlesque act in the Vienna Boylesque Festival last year and won best classical repertoire." He blew the smoke in a circle.

"As time went by, I became one of the resident burlesque performers at a theatre here in Rome. But you'll be surprised that people still consider burlesque performance taboo because it involves nudity!" Fabrizio lit a second cigarette.

The following night, Fabrizio invited me for dinner at his

place. He cooked homemade pasta for us based on a family recipe from southern Italy.

"Have a look." He showed me videos of his burlesque performances while preparing the dish.

"I don't like to perform at the gay clubs. It's difficult to get appreciation from the audience because they don't understand the concept of burlesque. They judge me solely on my skinny body and expect a muscular go-go boy performance." He stopped chopping the garlic and looked at me.

We ate together in the living room once the food was served; *penne Napoletana* with feta, olives and parsley.

"Speaking of food, I also organised the smallest burlesque show in the world," he mumbled as he chewed his pasta. "I combined the art of Italian food and burlesque performance. I invited no more than 15 people to come to my living room. At the start, the audience ate my homemade dishes while getting to know each other. Then I performed in front of them as dessert. The idea was to share the intimacy within a small group." He put down his plate and showed me his shimmy, bump and grind movements.

Spending time with my fellow boylesque performers helped me understand what it took to present the art of teasing on the stage. It is like Italian pasta; burlesque requires passion and flavour in order to taste warm and comforting.

***

I continued my journey from Rome to Vienna with two suitcases, equal to the $300 excess baggage I'd paid at Perth airport. One was for the burlesque costumes, including two unicorn headpieces and a giant teddy bear, and the other was for my daily outfits. The train became the cheapest transportation option to take me and my belongings across European land. But travelling on the train to Austria via Munich required extra caution. The police officer conducted an identity check for every passenger at the border due to the massive influx of Syrian refugees into Austria at the time.

"Can I see your passport, please?" A rugged man in a military uniform came to my seat.

I checked my pocket and realised I'd put it in the small bag. "Sorry, my passport is in my luggage."

He followed me to the storage section at the end of the wagon. There were a couple seconds of stillness as the officer reviewed my document.

"Thank you!" He smiled at me after seeing my sparkly burlesque costumes and cock pouch inside the suitcase.

After a four-hour journey from Munich, I arrived in Vienna just in time for a welcome dinner organised by the producer of the Vienna Boylesque Festival, Jacques. As a well-known burlesque artist himself, he wanted to create a safe space before the festival began, and welcome all the performers who had travelled from different parts of the world. Once more, I checked the reflection of my leopard-print leggings in the restaurant window before I entered.

"I really appreciate the opportunity to perform at your festival. It means a lot to me." I hugged Jacques when I got to the dinner table.

I sat in the available seat in the corner of the room. During dinner, I positioned myself as a newcomer who was making his international festival debut.

"How is the burlesque scene in New York?" I asked the performer next to me.

"I'm a resident artist at a local bar," he answered. "We only get paid through tips, but that can be a lot on busy weekend nights."

My initial nervousness about breaking the ice had dissipated. The warm atmosphere at the dinner made me feel welcome, as we were not there for the competition. It was a bunch of creative people gathering over food and plenty of alcohol. Most of them were full-time performers and had been in the burlesque scene for years. I was flattered to be surrounded by recognised burlesque artists who had won international awards and toured the world.

"Me? Oh well, I'm a long way from your achievements and skills." I sipped my gin and tonic to boost my confidence. "I'm just a baby who entered the burlesque scene four months ago. A fierce unicorn burlesque baby, to be exact." I placed my index finger on top of my head to indicate a horn.

***

The performance day had finally arrived. I got to the venue early to do a technical run. Each performer was given time to play their track and check the lighting. While the crew tested it, I was mesmerised by the beautiful interior design of the theatre that was built in 1870. I stood there, looking at the empty seats that would be packed in a matter of hours. I closed my eyes and took in the energy of the stage. I envisioned myself conquering the European audience for the first time.

The backstage area was enormous, with a dressing table and mirror for each artist. I shared the preparation space with the 21 other performers and was the only Asian on the festival's second night. While the others put on their make-up and sorted out their costumes, I looked in the mirror to finally admit to myself that I was an artist, a title that I had believed was just a hobby as a result of growing up in Indonesia. Being an artist was not something I had pursued as a child's dream. It was all about being an engineer, doctor or police officer because those things were deemed to provide a stable income.

Getting ready backstage that night was a significant privilege, and I credited my unicorn alter-ego, who had taken me so far. Even without an art education background or extensive performance experience, I was there with many high-calibre artists. They were brave, creating a different world on the stage and pouring their energy out, despite the risk that the world would not appreciate their craft. I adored their heart of art.

One of the performers came up to me. "Hello, fellow Aussie!"

I could not hide my smile at being called an Australian and gave him a warm hug in return. He was Mr Boylesque Australia 2014, who resided in Berlin. I'd attended his boylesque introduction class in 2015, where he taught me how to strip off a suit in a burlesque style.

"Look at this picture. I wondered what you had been up to since the workshop. But here you are!" He scrolled through his Instagram account and showed me the group photos he'd taken at the time.

The festival host, World Famous Bob, a neo-burlesque icon, approached each participant to confirm the introductory script she would read on stage.

"I believe in the unicorn spirit too! My bedroom is dominated by the colour pink and unicorn images." She grabbed my hand. "Okay, darling, this is what I got for your introduction. All good?" She showed me a cue card.

"Yes, that's perfect! Just a minor comment from me. I want

the audience to know that I am originally from Indonesia, even though I currently represent Perth, Australia. You know, here people see burlesque as an art form, but in Indonesia, they would see it as pornography. I want the audience to realise that I have to cross the sea to find a safe place to perform as a unicorn."

I presented my act, "The Dark Side of the Unicorn", at the end of the first half before intermission. It was initially created for a Halloween party to show the audience that even a unicorn had a dark side—grotesque revenge. It is the only place one can see when they reach the tipping point of jealousy, where sweetness becomes bitterness, and tears become thick blood.

The performance started when I danced with a giant teddy bear to a romantic song, "Something Stupid", by Nicole Kidman and Robbie Williams. As the melody changed, I put him on the chair and walked away to grab a bucket of flowers. The audience was utterly silent when the track turned into dark techno music at the start of the prologue: "I need a little darkness to get me going."

I stripped off my black skirt and walked behind the teddy bear. I grabbed the red roses, tore them apart, and threw them in the air as the epilogue said, "I'm ready to shine."

The rest of my choreography was about kinky moves. I slapped the teddy bear and spat on him. I pulled his head and stood on it with my high-heeled boots. It was the fetish scene I'd learnt in Berlin. I then took off my corset and shoulder feather before standing behind the teddy bear once more. I grabbed a vial of fake blood hidden behind him. And when it burst inside my palm, I spread it onto my face and chest. It was bold red, a warning for the viewers.

Poor teddy bear. I took a bondage rope and whipped it on the floor while walking around him. The music was getting faster, and I giggled while I tied his neck. When the song stopped and changed to the sound of a ringing bell. I hung him up and swayed him like a pendulum. I laughed out loud until my voice echoed throughout the whole room, and stared into the crowd. I dropped the teddy bear and dragged him along the floor as I exited the stage. No mercy.

The audience was in shock over what they had seen. The sound of clapping was lower compared to the performance before me. Maybe they thought they might come across as psychopaths if they cheered too loudly over the massacre of a teddy bear. The host moved back a few steps when she saw me covered in fake blood, and she had not expected a fluffy unicorn to kill an innocent teddy bear.

"Can I have a quick photo of you, please? It's for the magazine." A woman with glasses raised her camera at the backstage stairs. I posed for her against the wall with the teddy bear covered in blood before I returned to the changing room.

"Did you hear me scream during your act? That was amazing!" Mr Boylesque Australia 2014 came to the make-up table as I wiped my face during the intermission.

"I was so scared and kept wondering what was going to happen to that poor teddy bear," said one of the burlesque headline artists from New York.

After I cleaned myself, I sat at the back of the theatre to watch the second half of the performance.

"Are you from Jakarta?" An elegant lady with a feather boa on her shoulder turned towards me. "My close friend is actually from there."

The International Debut

I had not realised I was sitting next to the infamous burlesque legend Perle Noire, who won Best Debut at the Burlesque Hall of Fame in 2008. We had a brief conversation before the other performances started. Somebody noticed my background, and it was a well-known artist. It made my burlesque night complete.

"Ozak, well done on your performance!" My friend Lisa from Perth, who happened to be in Europe for a holiday, congratulated me after the show. All the performers mingled with the audience at the theatre bar after the festival.

"I had three favourite acts tonight. Yours was one of them," said a German man who came up to me with his wife.

"We actually organise a burlesque festival on a boat during springtime in Germany," said the wife. "You should come and perform there."

My joyous smile shone whenever I talked to people as I was overwhelmed by the feedback I received that evening. I proved to myself that I could still impress European audiences even without winning a competition title. The most important part was sharing my energy on the stage and letting it resonate with the crowd.

***

A couple of weeks after the performance, I sent a message to the producer to thank him for having me at the festival. I also asked him for feedback on my performance.

"*I think you should stick with the act based on the acceptance letter I sent you a couple of months ago,*" he wrote. "*I personally do not have a problem at all with what you performed at the festival, but it could be a problem for other producers.*"

I read the message a few times, as I was confused. For the

festival application, every performer submitted two acts. I chose "The Birth of the Unicorn" as my first preference and "The Dark Side of the Unicorn" as my second option.

"*The email I received was for me to perform 'The Dark Side of the Unicorn'. The rundown event backstage also mentioned 'The Dark Side of the Unicorn',*" I replied to him within minutes.

I was already in Lyon, France, continuing my European holiday while waiting for his reply. Performing in Vienna was my international debut, and I did not want to get in trouble because of my grotesque performance.

"*I am sorry. I admit that one of my crew copied and pasted the wrong link. I initially approved 'The Birth of the Unicorn', the pink fluffy one.*

My feedback for you has changed then. I like your vision and the concept of creating acts around your unicorn persona since there are not many unicorn burlesque performers out there. It is so good to have a contrast between the colourful pink act and the dark one." The producer inserted a smiley emoji and a love heart at the end of the sentence.

I was sitting by the Rhone River with a glass of champagne when I read the message. My holiday mood had calmed me down. Contacting the producer for feedback after the show turned out to be the right move, especially for a newbie performer like me. Otherwise, I would never have known there was a miscommunication.

"*Come back to Vienna next year, darling,*" Jacques added another message.

My heart was full of rich experiences after my international debut. I committed to maintaining relationships with people involved in the Vienna Boylesque Festival. I'd witnessed how the producer had successfully executed the event and, most importantly, provided a safe space for all performers. He treated us with immense respect and warmly welcomed us from the first until the last day we were there. My participation in the festival marked a significant milestone in my burlesque journey. I was no longer an orphanage artist as they had adopted me as part of their burlesque family.

21 THE REDUNDANCY

Nothing beautiful lasts forever. Soon after the euphoria of my international debut in Vienna, I received an email from my boss: *"Please get in touch with me once you are back from your holiday."* My intuition said I should prepare for the worst.

Taking two months of unpaid leave and travelling around Europe was bittersweet. I'd had incredible experiences through the cities I'd explored and the friends I'd met. But I'd burnt so much money during the oil and gas crisis, and it particularly hurt that the euro had exhausted my Australian dollar bills. To ease the guilt, I remembered the mantra, "You only live once."

"I had a great time, thanks! How can I help you?" I called my boss as soon as I returned to Perth.

"It has been a tough time lately with the oil and gas industry downturn…" He paused on the phone. "I am sorry to inform you that management must let you go. There is no personal motive here. I hope you understand."

In Indonesian culture, whenever we have bad news, we always find a way to say "at least" to ease the disappointment. In my circumstances, at least I already had my permanent residence status, which was more than enough reason to keep my head up. It did not hurt me as I'd known it was only a matter of time before I was made redundant.

"Thank you for letting me know." I maintained a soft voice as I spoke to him. "It must be hard to be in your position delivering this message repeatedly."

"You are taking it well. I argued with some senior engineers when I called them," he sighed.

"I would be keen to work with the company again if there is an opportunity in the future," I added.

"That is good to hear. I will let you know the exit interview date so you can come to the office to collect your stuff." He ended the phone call.

I executed my last day at work with style, wearing a beige-coloured suit and tie to attend the exit interview. I wanted to engrave a glorious ending and make a lasting impression, just like I had when I'd first joined the company.

"Sorry that we have to let you go." The Human Resources staff welcomed me to the meeting room. My boss was not in the office on the day of my exit interview.

"I actually want to thank the company for the fantastic opportunity to work here. I grew so much as a person." I placed both hands on the table and took a gentle bow.

"You will receive a full month's salary to cover the notification period and a redundancy package based on how many years you have been working with us." She handed me a piece of paper. "This is the total amount the company will pay you. Please review this document, then return the signed paper to me later." She pointed out the summary section.

My savings account had dried out after the Europe trip. When I saw the amount of my redundancy package, I almost jumped out of my chair. I could survive for the next couple of months without working. I rushed to my desk right after I signed the paper. A spontaneous idea crossed my mind to look up last-minute flights to Indonesia. I wanted to celebrate *Eid al-Fitr* with my family for the first time since I'd moved to Australia. It is a holy day for Muslims, marking the end of the fasting month.

It was one night before the *Eid al-Fitr* celebration. I knew it would be difficult to get a flight as many Indonesian expatriates would be returning home. But like a fairy tale, there was always a happy ending after the downfall. I managed to secure the last available seat.

"*Mum, I will fly from Perth this afternoon and arrive in Jakarta at midnight. I want to celebrate Eid al-Fitr with you all tomorrow morning.*" I sent a text to my mother. Just a week ago, I'd told her I could not return to Indonesia.

On my last day at work, I saw my colleagues sitting quietly at their desks, dealing with their emotions as they also had been made redundant. I did not want to interrupt their grieving. I focused on packing up piles of technical reports as evidence of my legacy. Every day working in the office had become an achievement until I'd reached the tipping point of redundancy. I only said goodbye to my colleague who sat next to me. We'd worked together on countless projects as the core engineering team in the drilling department. She followed me to the lift before I said a final farewell.

When I hugged her for the last time, I forgot how many times we'd argued about the smallest things, like the decimal points of the analyses' results. I forgot how we always corrected each other's grammar with a red pen in the project reports. I forgot how stressed we became when we found each other's mistakes in the software input. She was the only person who cried when I left the company; that was all I thought of when we hugged. After four years since the first time I stepped into the office building, she was the only one who walked with me to the lift and waved goodbye.

***

I had mixed feelings about going home after having the gayest two-month holiday in Europe. There was still pink glitter stuck in my hair from the unicorn headpiece. The next minute, I'd booked a religious trip back to Indonesia. My family already knew that I was gay since they'd found out about my participation in Mr Gay World, but we had never talked about it face to face. This *Eid al-Fitr* holiday could be the moment to have those tough conversations.

By the time I landed, my mind had shifted from hedonism to spiritualism. The airport was quiet when I finally arrived in Jakarta at midnight. Most people had travelled a week before the big day. Meanwhile, I was still searching for transportation to my hometown, 120 km from Jakarta. Just six hours before the celebration, I found a shuttle bus company that was operating last minute. I was scared to find I was the only passenger. The toll road between Jakarta and Bandung is notoriously spooky. Living in Australia had not made me any less superstitious. I'd grown up listening to horror stories about the tragic accidents that had happened on this road, and people had seen spirits in a particular spot on the highway.

"Please have some chocolate bread, sir." I handed the driver a box of food, hoping to break the silence and engage him in conversation to make sure he was a real person, not a ghost.

The exhaustion took me to sleep. My mum and dad hugged me when I arrived home at 3 am; they had waited for me all night. In the bedroom, I could hear people reciting *Takbir*, an Islamic Arabic expression, to praise Allah. It echoed from the mosque's loudspeaker and had been going the whole evening. It would stop in a few hours, just before the *Eid-al-Fitr* prayer started at 6.30 am.

"*Allahu akbar, Allahu akbar, Allahu akbar. La ilaha illallah, Wallahu akbar, Allahu akbar wa lillahil hamd.*"

"Allah is the greatest, Allah is the greatest, Allah is the greatest. There is no God but Allah. And Allah is the greatest, Allah is the greatest, and to Allah belongs all praise." I listened to those recitations as my lullaby.

The 6 am alarm woke me up, and my mum was already too excited to pick my outfit for the day.

"Cover your head with this." She insisted I should wear a religious headpiece to hide my alternative bun hairstyle. "It is inappropriate. You are about to pray to God."

I followed her order as I was too sleepy to argue. There was no sign of unicorn fabulousness on me. Like any other man who came to the morning prayer, my look had been transformed into one of uniformity.

My dad and I went to the mosque together to attend the *Eid al-Fitr* prayer. We stayed inside while the women prayed outside, using recycled newspapers to cover the street before laying the rugs on them. The procession for *Eid al-Fitr* is different from daily prayer as it requires two repetitions, and we have to recite *Takbir* seven times on each repetition. Even though I stopped praying after moving to Australia, I still remembered every word of it. I'd practised since I was five years old, and the struggles had always been the same, difficult to concentrate as the recitation was in Arabic. Random thoughts about food and unicorn burlesque performances occupied my mind. That morning, I prayed to Allah in my own language instead.

"*Dear Allah, it has been a while since I last worshipped you. A lot of things have happened. I am sure you have seen it from above too.*

"*Remember when I went to Mecca and prayed in front of the Kaaba? I was 14 years old and cried my eyes out to you. I said that I did not want to be gay, and I asked you for a miracle. In high school and university, I kept praying to be cured. I devoted my time to getting to know you by joining Islamic youth organisations. I prayed five times a day and sometimes woke up at 3 am for an additional prayer. But this same-sex attraction is still here.*

"*When I left Indonesia and started my journey in Australia, I felt like I grew apart from you. I wanted to know who I was, away from the religious boundaries I sometimes could not comprehend. But I always come back to you when I have trouble, and sometimes during my happiness too. I still say your name before I sleep because I am used to it. I spent my upbringing worshipping you, and look at me now. I've made my way back to the mosque just to see you again.*

"*Regardless of what I have been up to, I hope you allow me to say your name whenever I want and need to, even though I am not the best worshiper, according to some people. Can we just have a relationship between us? It won't be perfect, but I like to worship within my capacity. If you are the greatest, you must have the compassion to spare a spot next to you for people like me.*"

***

I asked my father for his forgiveness and vice versa after the prayer finished. It is a tradition during *Eid al-Fitr* to shake each other's hands, symbolising forgiveness, even to a stranger. I could still recognise familiar faces in the mosque. Seeing their presence brought back memories of when I used to go there at 4.30 am for *Subuh*, the first prayer of the day.

"Ozak, get married soon! What are you waiting for?" My neighbour approached me as I collected my sandals outside the mosque, and he said it out loud in front of my father.

My neighbour ordered me as if he was my parent. The saddest thing was that I could only reply with a bitter smile, knowing it was typical small talk in Indonesia. I was agitated deep down because I had not seen him for a decade, long before I moved to Australia, but that was the first thing he said to me. My father just laughed as he thought it was a common joke with an element of truth. I left the mosque abruptly to rescue myself. That moment added another reason to the list of why I did not want to live in Indonesia anymore. Everybody is always curious about someone else's life.

I went home to eat *ketupat*, a type of dumpling made from rice packed inside a diamond-shaped pouch of woven palm leaves. It is a typical food served with a spicy curry during *Eid al-Fitr*, and I had been craving it since I was on the plane.

"Come with me to greet and ask forgiveness to the neighbourhood," my mum interrupted when she returned from the mosque.

"I haven't seen them for years. What should I apologise for?" I defended my time eating the *ketupat*.

"If you do not show up, our neighbours will think you are snobbish," my mum warned.

I dragged myself to the surrounding neighbourhoods only because I cared about my family's reputation. I also visited the neighbour I'd met in the mosque that morning. He was an ex-journalist who used to live in Australia. I sat in his living room, only to hear about marriage again.

"I saw you on YouTube," he said to me.

I froze. I thought my neighbour was referring to the Mr Gay World videos.

"When you participated in the youth exchange program," he continued.

My mum and I were walking side by side as we left my neighbour's house. She broke her silence on the way back home.

"I always pray for you, so you can follow the right path. My heart is broken that you have become gay, something that is forbidden in our religion. I hope you get enlightened. Pray to Allah more often, my dear son. I hope Allah forgives you. There is always an opportunity for you to change anytime, for you to surrender. I can always help." Her voice trembled, and she looked at the ground, avoiding eye contact.

My parents did not understand the concept of "Love is Love" or "Born This Way". What they did understand was that I was supposed to get married to a woman and have kids. They feared I would be lonely as I got older, and that no one would take care of me.

"Forgive me, my dear son. It is not your fault that you have become gay. Life is an endless test, indeed. But there is always a clue for you to come back to the right path." She patted my back.

My mum is always the one who communicates with me, as my dad is a reserved man. He is a tough person from a province well known for its rough sailor men. Every time my mother makes conversation with me, there is the possibility that my dad has spoken about me to her first.

I looked at my mum as we returned to our house. I let out my thoughts that had been accumulating all this time, trying to convey my ideas in the vocabulary she was familiar with.

"Dear Mum, whose heart is broken. It is no one's fault. I've lived in my body all my life, so I know exactly how it feels to be gay. If you want to talk about religion, good deeds and sins, everyone is imperfect. The best person at the end of the day is the one who helps instead of harms others. Accepting gay people is a choice. In Australia, the government recognises our rights, even though some people believe in Christianity. That is why I moved there and left everything behind here. Mum, I've already made peace within myself about who I am. I just want to be honest with you.

"I promise that someday I will have a boyfriend. I will introduce him to you face to face. Perhaps it will change your perception once you meet someone who loves me. You want to see me happy, don't you?" I walked inside the house and left her on the veranda.

The conversation I had with my mother left me pondering. I am beyond religion. I see myself as a human first, before religious dogma, not the other way around. If I followed the entire Muslim practice, not only could I not be gay, but I would not also be able to perform burlesque on stage in Vienna, get naked at hippy festivals in Tasmania, go to an orgy party in Berlin, drink vodka at the Gay Village in Rome, shake hands with the opposite gender or even listen to pop music. All of those things would be *haram*, forbidden. My world would be a defining dash, where in reality, I like to colour outside the line.

As part of my identity-search journey, I treasure all the moments I was involved in Islamic youth organisations. But I am more interested in seeking life experience as a human. I do not want to see my belief in God as oppression; instead, I consider it my spiritual liberation. My faith is love, and I aim to spread kindness to my surroundings. And, I am sure. There will always be a space for me, space for all of us, including those non-believers, in this whole vast galaxy. All this time, our inner voice could be the God we have been searching for.

22 THE OPPRESSION

There is this feeling when home is no longer home. Some people call it loss; I called it unrequitedness. My home country, Indonesia, had made me feel like a second-class citizen due to my sexual orientation.

The oil and gas was not the only crisis of 2016. There was also a catastrophe within the LGBTQIA+ community in Indonesia. The Indonesian Minister of Higher Education banned LGBTQIA+ student organisations from the university. The Minister of Defence said LGBTQIA+ rights activism was more dangerous than a nuclear bomb. The Indonesian Psychiatrists Association labelled same-sex orientations and transgender identities as mental disorders. Some Indonesian politicians thought that having more than one wife was acceptable, but believed the LGBTQIA+ community was a serious threat to the country and should not be exposed publicly. The collective intolerance from government officials, radical Muslim organisations, and community groups led to an immediate breakdown of LGBTQIA+ human rights in Indonesia.

I was unemployed after being made redundant, but it did not stop me from joining a burlesque competition for the second time. When the oppressors used words for their invasion, I chose performance art as my weapon to protest the situation in the place I used to call it home. There was no motivation for fame. Instead, it was an opportunity to present a new act, "Do Not Take Away My Horn", to depict the struggles people like me, breaking the chain of pain.

It was a rainy evening in September 2016 when the boylesque competition started at a theatre in the suburb of Fremantle. On the opening night, all five contestants had to strut on a red carpet in our best glamorous Hollywood outfits prior to presenting our acts. I appeared in a full tuxedo with a unicorn horn on my head. Under the stage lighting, I froze for a second to close my eyes and listen to the excitement of the audience. It was my moment to conquer. My right hand reached for the horn, not to salute the crowd, but to jerk off in a gesture to my oppressors a thousand miles away.

I returned backstage to prepare for my performance. My costumes and props were arranged next to a fellow burlesque artist, Kenjai, who also has an Asian background. I had additional mental support by having her beside me, which I did not have in the previous competition year. This time, I did not feel so alone backstage.

"Use this glue for your pasties!" Kenjai passed me a tube as we sat in the corner of the room, getting ready for our act.

All the elements of my performance represented the agony of marginal people searching for freedom. My primary costume was made of leather, and *Shibari* ropes were used to restrain my chest, arm, and head. The kinky fetish bondage gave me muscle pain while I waited for my name to be called. Every discomfort helped me to build the performance mood, dark and cold. The more I felt the physical ache, the more I could intensify the emotion of being oppressed. This time, there was no joyful pink fluffy unicorn. This time, it was about anger and outcry, with no room for me to smile.

The spotlight shone as I started my performance. The choreography began with a piano version of "Creep" by Radiohead. I stood on stage with my wrist tied to a horizontal wooden plank on my back, as if I was being crucified. Five ropes were attached to each side of the block, creating a flowy effect when it swung. I carried my props onto the stage as a symbol of my burden.

"Arrrggghhh!" I screamed until I tensed my throat, unleashing the rope on my hand.

The audience started to recognise the emotion I was trying to deliver. They cheered when I took off my leather shirt. But I was in the world of oppression; I did not perform for crowd pleasure. I grabbed another rope on my body as it symbolised the maltreatment. Blood rushed through my arms as I untied it. It was not a graceful burlesque movement, rough when I used the rope to whip the stage as a sign of fighting back. One, two and three, I counted my steps to the front of the stage. People were staring into my eyes. In my mind, they were the oppressors who laughed out loud and spat in the face of the LGBTQIA+ community in Indonesia. When "Yellow Flicker Beat" by Lorde played, I pointed my index finger towards my horizon. I marked them, one by one, with my deepest eye contact, remembering the words of hypocrisy coming from the oppressors' mouths.

The lighting changed to red as I crawled on the floor, reaching the unicorn horn inside the box. I cried as soon as I crowned myself with it. It reminded me that I had finally found my identity. I had gained independence in the war against the tyrants. I broke the wood in half to close the act, signifying the end of the oppression against people like me.

There is always a temptation to taste the glory of the competition, especially after giving everything I have on stage. But burlesque is a microphone to showcase my voice; I am not chasing the title anymore. I had put aside my desire to win the title long before I started the competition.

"The runner-up will receive the title of Mr Boylesque Perth 2016. Congratulations to Tess OZteron!" The host called my alter-ego name.

I went up to the stage and hugged the host. The audience cheered me up with an explosion of clapping. I looked out at them and hoped that I was representing someone's voice and feelings that evening. I believed there would be people who could relate to my stories, personal experiences, and raw emotions while I was on stage. It was not often I got a chance to appear in a big crowd just to be heard.

***

"Ozak, do you want to perform your burlesque act at our event?" Desi, my Indonesian friend who'd recently migrated to Australia, called me a couple of weeks after the competition. "We will organise a fundraising event in Melbourne for the Indonesian LGBTQIA+ community who is currently under oppression!"

Desi and I had known each other since senior high school. Back then, I'd joined a Muslim vocal group, and she wore a hijab. Our paths started to diverge at university. I became a radio announcer and joined the international backpacker community, while she became a tattooist artist and was heavily involved in the local punk scene. Both of us had our own battle with Islam, and the current situation in Indonesia had reunited us as LGBTQIA+ allies.

"Stay at my place," Desi offered by phone. "It's a squatting house in Collingwood."

"Squatting?" I imagined the toilet style widely used in Indonesia.

"It's an abandoned property, but my friends and I occupy the building and have been living here for a couple of months." She paused for a second to wait for my comment.

I lowered my voice. "Is it safe?"

"The police have visited a couple of times to evacuate us because they want to demolish it for a road project. But that was ages ago. You will be fine here!"

I imagined an abandoned property to be like a haunted place. But when I arrived, I ended up staying longer than planned as there was hot water, electricity, and Wi-Fi, and it was close to the gay bars in Collingwood. I also went to a squatting warehouse, where some of Desi's friends from the punk community lived, for a rehearsal the day before the fundraiser. The rooms were made from plasterboard, and it had facilities such as a communal kitchen and a printing space for digital arts. Booklets regarding anti-racism, and anti-discrimination over sexual orientation, gender and religion were displayed on the table next to the printers. I learned that a marginal group like them had teamed up with other minority groups to support the equality cause.

"Welcome to our fundraising night to support the LGBTQIA+ community in Indonesia." The host, wearing a gothic outfit, pulled the microphone away as her voice dominated the bar.

It was 9 pm, and the dance floor was already flooded with LGBTQIA+ allies. Hundreds of local queer people had flocked to the venue to support the cause. A total of ten artists were performing voluntarily as part of their contribution. The explosive audience reaction boomed in the music hall every time the performers presented their talents. It psyched me, but I had to control my heartbeat as I was the last artist in the line-up. Not only did I present "Do Not Take Away My Horn", but I had also prepared a final act for that evening. After finishing my boylesque performance, I invited a guitarist to accompany me. I was still covered with fake blood, and was wearing only my thong and chest harness bondage ropes.

"Just a couple of hours before this show, a gay couple in Indonesia got arrested for uploading their kissing photo on social media. I have created a special song for tonight. This melody is dedicated to all the unicorns in Indonesia who are still fighting against oppression!"

Then I sang my own song, "Like a Unicorn", to the public for the first time.

"I found the magic in me. It glows my soul like a unicorn.
Above the rainbow after the rain, I rise and shine, light up in the dark.
I broke the chain of pain. Born to be real, cannot be changed.
From darkness into light, I live to love, like a unicorn."

All the effort from ticket and artwork sales had raised a thousand dollars. The organiser donated the money to one of the LGBTQIA+ non-profit organisations in Indonesia. The audience also gave positive feedback about my original song. It motivated me to record it in a music studio in Perth to reach a wider audience, especially in Indonesia. One more time, I blew my savings in the middle of unemployment.

"Two days of recording will cost a thousand dollars, which is a special deal!" The music producer replied to my email. *"Just send me your song sample so I can brainstorm the music concept."*

The producer and I collaborated on the arrangement, melody and harmonisation from the moment I stepped into his studio. It felt like a long-lost dream come true. My childhood memories flashed before my eyes as I remembered I wanted to be a singer. Time flew during the production, and the song was pretty much ready on the second day. I distributed the song independently through online portals and played it countless times as my lullaby.

The decision to record my music was the right move. I got the opportunity to showcase it on the local Perth radio. During the short interview with the announcers, I raised awareness among the Australian audience about the oppression in the Indonesian LGBTQIA+ community.

"Do you want to perform at Perth Pride?" An event organiser contacted me not long after my track was aired.

***

Camp Unicorn signed up to march at Perth Pride to support the same-sex marriage campaign during the controversial plebiscite in Australia. The parade was to take place just before the launch of my song. Around thirty people from our group came, and I stood on the boom box bike wearing a pink unicorn headpiece and holding a seven-inch dildo in my hand. We showed people in Perth that unicorns not only exist, but we also supported love to always win.

"Can you be spontaneous backup dancers for my single launch performance?" I asked my friends at the final marching destination.

Some other unicorns followed us to the venue where I

would perform. It was meant to be a ticketed event, but because I was one of the artists that night, the security let fifteen of them in for free.

It was a relaxing moment with my five dancers backstage. While we regained our energy, I discussed the dance formation we would do over the foods and drinks provided by the organiser. Suddenly, the unicorn groupies came backstage. "Woohoo, free drinks!"

There was no security to prevent backstage access. I was starting to get stressed out about my upcoming performance. At the same time, I had to deal with them as they kept coming and freeloading the alcohol provided for the artists.

"Ozak, you need to do something about your people. Otherwise you could damage your reputation," Kenjai, my burlesque friend, warned me.

"Would you mind asking them to leave? Please?" I grabbed her hand, showing her how desperate I was to focus on my performance preparation.

The time passed by with the chaos backstage. I stood in the corner, clearing my mind until it was finally showtime. I performed the pink fluffy unicorn burlesque act first, which I had done plenty of times. There was no issue, except I only had a minute break before the singing performance.

"This song is dedicated to the Indonesian LGBTQIA+ community currently being oppressed by the government and radical Muslim organisations."

I struggled to catch my breath at the first verse, too exhausted from the marching and high-energy burlesque dancing. I needed more than a minute break to gather my Zen. The situation worsened; I could not hear my voice from the stage clearly as the speaker was positioned towards the audience. I could feel that I was singing out of the key during the modulation. Cold sweat dripped down my face, imagining how embarrassed I would be if I were in the crowd to hear myself singing like that.

Something had to be done to cover my breathing and singing issues. I interacted with my backing dancers instead and came up with a synchronised dance. It became theatrical as we moved around the stage, interpreting the lyrics. My five talented friends managed to lift up the performance's energy. The unicorn groupies, who had trespassed backstage, also created a collective dance movement in the front section of the dance floor. They brought the crowd to life and eased my singing concerns on stage. They made me stressed and happy all at once.

I returned backstage once I'd finished my performance. Despite all the fun of being surrounded by my unicorn tribe, I was still devastated about the quality of my singing. I'd really wanted to deliver the song as best as possible because it meant the world to me.

"Congratulations on your performance! I enjoyed it a lot," said a female artist who had performed earlier.

"I sang out of tune, and I embarrassed myself." I covered my face.

"As an artist, sometimes we punish ourselves for things we thought were imperfect. Do not be too hard on yourself. Be kind. You've already inspired many people out there. If the LGBTQIA+ in Indonesia saw your performance tonight, they would be proud of you. Pride is about protest, and you did it in your own unicorn way." She comforted me with the best advice I could ever have received that night.

23 THE INVITATION

I always thought citizenship was an absolute status, and the only way to obtain it was through the inheritance of my parents. But reality had opened my eyes. Indonesia was no longer a safe space for me after the Indonesian government and community groups had invaded the LGBTQIA+ community. I became an outcast just because of a single parameter called homosexuality. And my survival instinct popped out; it was time to find a new home.

Australia had turned out to be a country where I could be authentic. It became the land that accepted me for who I was. And I wanted to be part of it, putting my roots down in Australia. The eligibility to apply for citizenship came after living in Australia for four years and holding a permanent residence visa for one year. I had an important decision to make before submitting the citizenship application to the Department of Home Affairs. Indonesia does not recognise dual citizenship. I would have to strip away a part of me to begin a fresh existence as a new human of Australia. I win some, I lose some.

The invitation to attend the citizenship assessment came within a couple of weeks. The test covered three topics: Australia and its people; Australia's democratic beliefs, rights and liberties; and government and the law in Australia. I read the modules repeatedly like I was learning a history subject at school. Some practice questions were specific: *"What happened in Australia on 1 January 1901?"* or *"Which official symbol of Australia identifies Commonwealth property?"*

"You have 45 minutes to complete the test. The pass mark is 75 per cent, so you only need to answer 15 out of 20 questions correctly." The officer welcomed me to the citizenship test centre and gave me brief instructions.

An old man was doing the assessment before me, and the officer told me he had failed three times. The pressure was on when I sat in the cubicle and read the multiple-choice questions on the computer. Every answer would lead me towards my citizenship destiny. I finished within 10 minutes, and the monitor showed the results at the end of the session: *"100 per cent correct!"*

The invitation letter for my citizenship ceremony arrived a month after I attended the test. It was a sacred piece of paper that came from Stirling Local Council and carried the hope of my new identity.

"Please bear in mind that you are not an Australian citizen until you take the oath. Furthermore, you can invite two guests to the ceremony."

There was an endless list of people that had made my Australian journey meaningful. But I had two weeks to choose who would witness my big day. The first guest slot went to my best friend, Nadia, whom I'd met in Indonesia back in 2008. She'd helped me a lot when I was a poor student trying to survive in the city of contrasts, Jakarta. We'd spent countless sleepless nights expending our early-twenties energy on the dance floor. She knew of my sexual orientation when I was still in the closet and had accompanied me to the gay club for the first time.

Nadia had relocated to Perth after getting her Australian working holiday visa and had come to the Blazing Swan with me. We'd never thought we would both end up in Australia, living in the same city again. We reunited in Perth as Indonesian immigrants who wanted to survive in a foreign land. Inviting Nadia was my glimpse of home. She reminded me of all the nostalgic memories in Indonesia, so I would not forget where I came from.

***

There was the second spot on the citizenship ceremony guest list. This one was special, dedicated to my complicated lover who had been quietly in the background of my immigration journey. Beyond my diverse circle of friends and outside my time as a performer, my heart had found refuge with a man called Fernando.

I had been longing for a love life in Australia but had had no luck finding the right person on gay dating apps until we'd crossed paths at the beginning of 2015. It was the year I visited Indonesia to collect my Indonesian police clearance for my permanent residence visa requirements.

"I am from Puerto Rico, and I lived in Indonesia for two years," he said at our initial encounter over weekend brunch.

Fernando, a warm Latino man with a rugged muscular build, intrigued me. He was the first person I'd met through an online dating app without kissing and having sex on the first date. It was just a hug that left my shirt smelling of his manly, woody aroma. I had to wait a week to see him for the second time. We finally held hands in the cinema, and it felt just right. I did not care about the ending of the film anymore. I was more interested in finding out what would happen between us after leaving the movie theatre.

"It was a fun night. Thank you for dropping me home." I unbuckled my seat belt. I looked at him closer as my intention was clear; I wanted him so bad. Inside the car, he let me kiss just for the touch of his lips, a flash of a couple seconds. It created an uproar inside my head, questioning why I did not get enough of him at that moment.

Then there was the green light I had been waiting for. Fernando invited me to his place two weeks after we met. My feelings towards him bloomed day by day. He introduced me to a new sensation when we sat on the couch next to the open window. I could feel the breeze against my ear, whispering to me to move closer until his thigh touched my jeans. The dim lights from candles on the table lit the living room with the help of the moonlight. Despite the darkness, I could still see his sharp jaw; a scruffy man wearing glasses. We were talking, but my heart was dancing. Every time he smiled, it shortened my breath. That was when I knew I wanted to grab him wholeheartedly. Three hundred and thirty-six hours after I heard his accent for the first time, we finally undressed each other in bed, feeling skin to skin.

We often met over lunch as our offices were nearby. We connected through various conversational topics such as culture, religion and work. I enjoyed having a chat with him, and I was attracted to his physique. But there was one hurdle when we initially met. He had been through a tough break-up.

"I'm not ready for a relationship," said my Puerto Rican lover. "My boyfriend left me when I came out to my wife."

Fernando was a married man with three kids, and his family lived overseas. I came into his life when he was fragile, and that was his baggage. I entered his personal space when he was dealing with the consequences of coming out, including the catastrophe of getting divorced.

It was not an ideal set-up for someone like me who had been longing for love. I had my own baggage as a loner gay man living in a foreign land. It was like a rabbit hole; no matter how busy I was with friends, I often returned to bed feeling isolated and empty in a lonely shadow. I saw the light when I was with him, someone I would rather be when I went to sleep. I saw comfort and intimacy, so I kept chasing him.

It took me a while to understand his situation. He rarely shared his family matters with me in detail, and I did not want to push him to open up. I respected his privacy. What I saw was a disparity. We felt like a romantic sanctuary whenever we spent the night together. I was convinced he was the person I had been waiting for in my life. But every time he travelled overseas to take care of his children, he would return to Perth as a cold-hearted man. He would disappear, without texting and calling, and build a wall protecting his broken heart. I would then need to climb the barrier, approaching him as if we just had met. I would wait days for a reply text to initiate a non-sexual catch-up, hold his hand until he allowed me to kiss him again, and remind him how good it was when we were together in our oasis.

I did not demand Fernando acknowledge our relationship; it was never about the label. In a lonely city, he was the most compatible person I thought I could be with. My Puerto Rican lover had witnessed all the big moments of my immigration journey in Australia.

"I am proud of you, man. You should definitely have been in the top ten!" Fernando said when I showed him footage of me in Mr Gay World.

Before we went to sleep, we often watched Miss Universe videos, as beauty pageant competitions are huge in Puerto Rico. "You should join the pageant again. I can be your coach!"

Fernando understood Indonesian culture. I often shared stories about my family and friends back there. He spoke Indonesian, which allowed him to connect with me even more.

"Sorry you had a stressful time at your sister's wedding. It reminds me of my driver in Indonesia. He invited me to his son's wedding who lived in the village. Everyone wanted to take a photo of me because I was the only foreigner there." He commented on my family pictures.

Fernando became my mentor. He listened to my complaints about the little things at work and enlightened me with career advice. He understood my struggles as he was a director in the oil and gas company.

"The crisis is going to get worse," he told me once, before I was made redundant. "You should keep chasing your boss, asking if you can help him in any way. Hopefully your company can sponsor your permanent residence visa knowing that you are valuable to them."

The most important part of our dynamic was that he accepted me as a burlesque performer. I was hesitant initially to show him my first appearance as a fluffy pink unicorn considering he was such a macho Latino man. But Fernando embraced my double life; the engineer he'd first met and the radical unicorn with its costumes and glitter.

"You are fearless! If I'd met you initially wearing pink high-heels and fur, perhaps it would have been too confrontational for me. But I like you as a person, and I support you." Fernando talked about my first burlesque performance video.

The thing about being a unicorn was, there was a side of me on stage where I rarely felt nervous. It could be that I was under the spell of my alter-ego, excited to let out my unheard voice as a protest in an art form. But every time I finished performing, my mood went down a spiral to transform me into an introvert. I poured my emotions out to the audience, and nothing was left by the end. That was when I enjoyed his company the most. Fernando helped me to find my equilibrium. I would go to his place just to be beside him in solitude. I'd cuddle him even when he'd already fallen asleep. My Puerto Rican lover was my calibration after I performed. A sweet simplicity.

Fernando often said to me, "You deserve someone better. You should find a boyfriend."

But I stayed and stood by him instead of walking away. I did not want to give up on love. I was the man who had crossed the ocean to find a better life and also to find love. I was used to being persistent.

Fernando treated me like a boyfriend. He always opened the car door before I got in, picked me up after work and cooked for me. He supported my burlesque performance by dropping me off at the venues and brainstorming performance ideas. He allowed me to stay at his place when I had to leave my shared house at the end of the lease. We spent countless nights watching *Friends*, and going to the cinema, beach and restaurants. We exercised together at the gym as part of our weekend routine. Fernando was a boyfriend without a label. I accepted that he did not want an official title because we were already living it day by day without him admitting it.

"This is not right. I don't want to hurt you. I wished you had come into my life earlier," Fernando said once. "Things would have been different."

"These are your clothes. This will be the last moment I see you," I said to Fernando on another occasion.

There were several times when we said goodbye. But love is an absurd concept. There were always moments that brought us back together. We found ways to reunite and build a deeper connection when that happened. Fernando had witnessed my darkest moments, and for that, I wanted him to see my brightest.

The invitation to the citizenship ceremony reflected my life that ran parallel with the connection with the people I'd met on the journey. All the characters had woven unique stories into each chapter of my immigration adventure. But amongst all the finest humans I had encountered, my Indonesian best friend and Puerto Rican lover were the figures who best represented my friendship and love life in Australia.

24 THE CEREMONY

Self-discovery is a non-linear journey, a soul-searching safari. I never would have migrated across the ocean to live as an openly gay man if I had not picked up the clue from the Pink Power Ranger. I did not think submitting the application form for the youth exchange program would open my horizons about Australia. I was not sure that searching for freedom in the hippy festival would give me the strength to march my own pride at Sydney Mardi Gras. I did not believe I could score a graduate job in an engineering company without local experience and education, and secure permanent residency. I did not know there was a tribe like Camp Unicorn, whose love would allow me to step onto stage in Mr Gay World and in my many burlesque performances. And I did not expect there would be a Puerto Rican man who would one day touch my heart. Those were the scattered dots in my life path that somehow created serendipity.

Self-discovery always starts from a single point and forms a sporadic connection somewhere at some specific time. In my case, it led me to this grand moment, the citizenship ceremony.

It was early evening in the City of Stirling, February 2017. A performance of "I am Australian" started the ceremony, a song I'd sung with the Australian delegates during the Australia Indonesia Youth Exchange Program. The melody serenaded a hundred new citizens and their guests. It stimulated goosebumps when the singer sang the chorus with her powerful voice, balancing the piano crescendo. Tears were in my eyes, as every note reminded me of the anfractuous immigration path I'd taken. Until the melancholic atmosphere was shattered.

"Waaaaaa!" A baby inside the hall cried, stealing the thunder.

The ceremony continued with a speech from the mayor talking about his parents' migration to Australia. "It was not easy to settle in a new country. But here you are!"

I read the booklet containing the list of new citizens and wondered how they were feeling. My Indonesian citizenship status was about to be stripped away once I pledged the oath. I counted down every second until my turn, nervous.

"Arozak Salam."

I went up to the podium as the host called my name. The officer read the pledge for me to follow and gave me two oath options, whether to be sworn under God or without. The peak of my immigration adrenaline culminated in that moment.

"From this time forward, under God, I pledge my loyalty to Australia and its people, whose democratic beliefs I share, whose rights and liberties I respect, and whose laws I will uphold and obey," I said.

"Congratulations!" The mayor shook my hand. An officer standing beside the stage gave me an Australian gold coin as a present before I got back to my chair. My mind floated around the hall while waiting for others to execute their pledges. I was happy that I'd become Australian, but also sad, as I had just officially lost my Indonesian nationality. Once upon a time, I was the Indonesian youth ambassador who had kissed a red and white flag before I'd left the country.

My pondering led me to Facebook land. I uploaded my photo holding an Australian citizenship certificate and wrote a status dedicated to my mother: *"Mum, I always believed that citizenship is a legacy you gave me. When I waved goodbye to you before I got on the bus, I never thought I would have the opportunity to change my citizenship one day.*

Mum, I discovered that citizenship is something I could earn. I finally got it tonight. I chose the place I belong because I do not like the feeling of being something in between. I was not meant to live in a grey area. I have found the land that allows me to be me with my full colour, bright and sparkling. It is here, in Australia.

Mum, I love you from across the ocean."

My friend Clara, from Camp Unicorn, commented on the post: *"Yeah! You are one of us!"*

Getting citizenship was my biggest immigration achievement, marking my new identity in a new life chapter. I proudly announced my Australian citizenship status to my family and friends as if it was my second coming out. I am a new human of Australia. Like the song lyrics in "I am Australian", I am a free man; I became Australian.

***

My whole immigration journey was about chasing the goal of staying permanently. When I woke up the day after I got my citizenship, all I felt was the void. I had achieved climax, which got me thinking about what was next. I contemplated my personal life and career. It was scary to do so. It always starts with emptiness, and then all the thoughts become heavy.

It is paramount to have a goal; important not to wake up

feeling stagnant. My initial step was looking for full-time work across Australia since I had been made redundant. But the oil and gas crisis was getting worse. Many of my good friends had returned to their home countries because they'd lost their jobs. The challenging economic situation also affected Fernando, my Puerto Rican lover.

"I need to move to Singapore to take care of my kids, and I got a temporary job contract there," he said over dinner after his company made him redundant. "Feel free to stay in my apartment while you sort out your plans." He held my hands.

There were numerous mornings that I'd wake up at 4 am because my Puerto Rican lover had an early flight on the weekend. But it was a restless night before he left Perth for good. We made love before the alarm rang so I could reserve the smell of his body. I savoured the last memories of his scruffy chin, his solid arms, the roughness of his hairy chest, and how he looked at our reflection in the mirror when he held me from behind.

I was still in bed, and I heard the sound of the shower running as he got ready to go to the airport. I was scared; it meant the taxi would pick him up in half an hour, and he would be gone soon. I pulled him to the bed once he dressed so I could hug him again, indulging in the scent of his cologne.

"Thank you for the time we shared together over the past two years. *Te quiero mucho.* I love you so much." He kissed me on the forehead when I walked him to the front door.

Fernando texted me on the way to the airport: *"Keep dreaming. Never let others define who you are. In moments of fear and doubt, just look back at the moment you bravely came to Australia to pursue your dreams. Think of all you did back then and how you succeeded!*

You can do it again, and again, and again. In the end, life is just a carousel.

Please remember that I will always be here for you. To listen, comfort, and support you. I am only one text message away. Thanks for all you have done for me. I will always be grateful. Love you."

Just when I had a new identity as an Australian, everything that mattered to me—my job, friends, and lover—was starting to disappear.

My personal circumstances had shaken my path to redefine what I wanted to do in life. I started to think about what it meant to be Australian. I wanted to say to the world that I was Australian, even though I was not born there, did not have an Australian accent, and looked Asian. I found the answers through the youth mobility program for Australians under 30 years old. It was essentially a working holiday visa to gain life experience in different countries. I considered it an opportunity to travel the world and represent my new country on a microscale. It was my way of reclaiming my fresh identity.

I was at the edge of the age requirements to apply for a one-year working holiday visa that allowed me to work, study or travel. I chose Spain as my destination to further improve my Spanish after having a Puerto Rican lover. It was an ambitious goal, and I also planned to continue the journey to the UK for a similar youth mobility program. Unlike any other country, young Australians could live there for two years. There I was, planning to be away from Australia for three years on a working holiday visa.

As soon as my Spanish visa was granted, I shrank all my belongings that had accumulated over the past six years. Those nostalgic items were hard to let go of because my melancholic soul loved to collect memories. A song by Miley Cyrus called "Malibu" became my soundtrack to accompany the decluttering process, and its lyrics reminded me of my Puerto Rican lover. I let myself be emotional while transforming everything I had into one piece of luggage for my daily outfits and two boxes of costumes I shipped to Barcelona in case I continued performing in Europe.

The last impression counted. My friend painted a picture of Fernando and me on a canvas, so I could leave it in his apartment before I left. I wrote a farewell message to him on the back of the painting.

"The hardest part is not the farewell words but missing the time we shared together. With you, those little things became so precious.

You are not afraid of who I am, with and without make-up. You see me as me. You have seen what people cannot see, and you often comforted me. This weirdo is already missing you. I am so blessed to have you in my absurd life. Thanks for your existence; you have touched my life."

My arrival in Melbourne on my Indonesian travel document back in 2011 had led me to a departure from Perth International Airport using the dark blue Australian passport. My longing for a permanent address back then had resulted in another immigration journey to Europe. How bizarre to think that life is cyclical; that my finishing line was also my starting point.

I put my seatbelt on as the plane was about to take off. It was a busy flight. My back-row seats were fully occupied.

"Holiday time?" The woman next to me took off her shawl and started the conversation.

"Even better!" I adjusted my seat. "I am going to live in Barcelona for a year!"

"Oh wow. That's awesome!" She leaned forward, showing her dimpled smile.

"How about yourself?" I looked at her.

"I will be visiting Ibiza!" She raised her hands in the air.

"So," she said. "Where are you from?"

I pondered. "I am from…"

ACKNOWLEDGMENTS

I wrote this book for you. It all started when I worked the night shift at a call centre in Barcelona in 2017, at the quietest time after midnight when the users in the Asia Pacific were still sleeping. I continued my manuscript in London, many nights before I slept next to my ex. Then the pandemic happened. I returned to Perth in 2020 to redirect my life and finish my book project. At midnight, exactly on my birthday in October, I submitted my manuscript to the publishers. No luck, I got countless rejections. So, I left the manuscript in the dust.

Fast forward to 2022, I joined the Australian Navy. I know, my life is random. A year and a half later, I decided to voluntarily discharge. Stories for another memoir. During my discharge process, I picked up my unfinished dream. I want to transform my manuscript into a book. I meant it. I did most of the work as a self-published author. I wanted to give this beauty to you. So, thank you for reading my book.

Thanks to my family and friends who exist in my day-to-day life. I also want to thank the people who are involved directly in the process of cooking my book. My editor, Johanna Craven. My photographer, Deric Martin. My graphic designer, Romain Gambetta. My supporter from day one who helped me with the initial editing and preparing my press release, Mikhalina Dombrovskaya. My test readers: Justin, Avery, Gloria, Geges, Audrey, Holly, and Clara. My beautiful people who helped me with the brainstorming process: Daz, Kenjai, Alda, Van, Fluff Family, and Kozzy. Many thanks to the people I have not mentioned who support me mentally without you realise it. Thank you, and thank you!

ABOUT THE AUTHOR

Arozak Salam is an Indonesian immigrant who previously lived in Jakarta, Barcelona and London. He is an aspiring writer, as well as a subsea engineer, burlesque performer, singer, LGBTQIA+ activist, alumni of the Australia Indonesia Youth Exchange Program and former Australian Navy Officer who graduated from the Royal Australian Naval College (New Entry Officers' Course 66).

www.ingramcontent.com/pod-product-compliance
Lightning Source LLC
Chambersburg PA
CBHW030254010526
44107CB00053B/1706